BELLERBY

A DALESEND VILLAGE

BELLERBY
A DALESEND VILLAGE

by

David S. Hall

Unicorn Projects

ISBN 0 9514639 0 X

First published, 1989
Second impression, 1994

Copies available
Unicorn Projects,
Unicorn House, Bainbridge,
Leyburn, North Yorkshire, DL8 3EH

Printed and bound by
SMITH SETTLE
Ilkley Road, Otley
West Yorkshire

Contents

	Acknowledgements	vi
	Foreword	vii
1	The Setting	1
2	Bellerby Takes Shape	6
3	"Howseling People"	11
4	Fields and Farming	20
5	Some Lords—	28
6	And Men	34
7	St. John's Church	40
8	Catholics and Nonconformists	49
9	The School	56
10	Earning a Living	66
11	Community Life	74
	Notes and references	81
	Index	91

Acknowledgements

This book was written to preserve something of the history which came to light during the course of a Workers' Educational Association evening class meeting in the village school at Bellerby from 1981 to 1985. The class was a joy to teach and its members a pleasure to know. Their kindness and enthusiasm, their willingness to participate, to lend and borrow material, and to be led into fieldwork contributed much to the success of the venture. They were, Noel Ashworth, Tom Berry, Jimmy Chilton, Mary Clarke, Tina Coates, Norman Crossley, Doreen Davy, Phil Gehrman, Tony Gregg, June Hall, Amy Hartley, Kathleen Hodgson, Ann Londsdale, Ida Lonsdale, Dick Metcalfe, Chris Peace, Joyce Peace, Geoff Pearson, Harry Petty, Alan Pratt, John Pratt, Maurice Pratt, Reg Ride, Ray Sayer, Liz Scott, Alan Shotton, Jo Shotton, David Thistlethwaite, Mary Thistlethwaite, Nora Thistlethwaite, Ken Thwaites, Ann Ward, Helen West, Ralph West, Ann Wheatley and Jim Wilkie.

The book owes a great debt to the owners and keepers of manuscripts, photographs, printed books and relics, and especially to those who have deposited material at the North Yorkshire County Record Office in Northallerton. Individual sources are identified in references and notes. We thank all those within and around Bellerby who gave us access to houses, land and farmbuildings. Also those not of the village who offered support, advice and co-operation. They include John Balmforth, Kaare and Irene Bergerud, Bob Ellis, Richard Gulliver, Shirley Kimble, Bill Parks, Margaret Ritchie and Ian Spensley. Marie Hartley and Joan Ingilby read the manuscript and wrote the foreword. My wife, June Hall, helped throughout. Patricia Rivron was instrumental in securing financial assistance from Richmondshire District Council and Marstons Brewery, and the Sayer family raised money in the village. I thank them all.

David S. Hall
Unicorn House
Bainbridge
1989

Foreword

In writing the history of Bellerby, our friend, David Hall, who lived there from 1980-1983, has joined the ranks of village historians. His study has been realised by extensive and careful research amongst the wealth of records associated with this comparatively small place, and in addition it has been helped by the co-operation of many people in Bellerby who have offered documents, memories and sometimes artefacts. For such a project the author has to be dedicated and profligate of his time, and in this case the result is a fascinating and sympathetic view of a village.

It begins in the mists of time with early man, followed by the appearance of the first written records which as the centuries pass increase in quantity until the picture emerges in sharp focus. The emphasis here is on people — the lords of the manor, yeomen, clerics, teachers, craftsmen, large and small farmers. It is sad that as usual few women, who were there through the centuries working without pause, stand out from the throng. One who does, Mary Morland, strikes a note of tragedy.

Readers of this story are offered a full account of Bellerby up to the present day. It will give pleasure to the inhabitants, and we think others will also find it of interest, especially in comparing the development and progress of the village with that of others that have had their histories researched and published. This is a valuable study of a village brought to light for posterity.

Marie Hartley and Joan Ingilby
1989

Note to the 1994 Edition

When this book was first published, four hundred copies were printed. Within eleven weeks, only a few copies were left. This reprint is produced in response to continued demand and with support from Barbara Craig. Sadly, it is as a memorial to David, who died in 1990. So, too, are the six pink-flowering horse chestnut trees and a plaque, placed on the village green by his former students, neighbours and friends.

June L. Hall
1994

1 The Setting

Like any English village, Bellerby is at the same time unique and commonplace. No story of a community in its setting over a thousand years and more can ever be told in its entirity. The evidence for a clear and perfect picture simply does not exist. Generations of people were born, lived and died without their presence being recorded; homes were built, rebuilt and dismantled without leaving a trace; and events took place which are beyond recall.

What can be gathered is a mass of fragments. Just as a few tiny pieces of a shattered pot can give an archaeologist a good idea of what the whole was like, so the shreds of evidence can be pieced together to make a pattern.

Documents, official records and personal papers, objects, past descriptions, old photographs, memories, maps, newspapers, buildings, field names, aerial photographs, customs, surveys, observations and a host more clues can be located, examined and checked for the part they have to play in the unfolding story.

The carved stone head which formerly graced the front wall of an old workshop in Bellerby Wynd. Its form is three dimensional with hair, ears and a mouth hole. It is perhaps a celtic cult object dating from the Iron Age.

Bellerby, a grey stone village at the moor-edge, between Swaledale and Wensleydale, has its own story to tell. Visitors flock in thousands to the more famous picture-postcard villages in the Dales, passing through Bellerby on the way from Richmond to Leyburn, or by-passing it altogether on the old Turnpike road from Richmond to Askrigg and beyond. There it nestles, at the foot of Runs Bank, amply rewarding the visitor who takes the time to walk round and look.

Here, in the Dales-end country, the landscape has a particular attraction — wide views across the Vale of Mowbray to the Cleveland and Howardian Hills, the nearer masses of East Witton Fell and Pen Hill across the valley of the river Ure; quiet farmland beyond the village; and above, the backdrop of heather moorland and stone walled pastures. In the village itself, Bellerby Beck and the Mill Beck diverted from it, race along through gardens and under stone bridges, cross the green and unite, eventually to join the river Swale.

Bellerby is situated one and a half miles north of Leyburn (nine miles from Richmond) on the A6108 in the Richmondshire District of North Yorkshire. The village, nestling in a shallow dip amongst low hills, stands at 750 feet O.D., with an open south-easterly aspect across gently falling ground backing up to windy moorlands in the north and west. Its houses straggle along the becks and the main road. Across the green the seventeenth-century Old Hall stands out amongst later buildings, and hints at the long story of the village.

This is largely limestone country. The double scarred Main Limestone of the Yoredale Series is the dominant rock of the district, though seldom seen on the surface, except in drystone walls and the impressive outcrops west of Leyburn. Quarries and limekilns below the Moor Road and west of the Manor House reveal this bedrock. Similarly, near Cross Head, the Ten Fathom Grit, overlying the Main Limestone, has been dug out and may be seen in drystone walls in the South Field. Higher rock beds on Bellerby Moor hold a thin seam of coal, once mined, among the sandstones which again were quarried, for millstones at a place called Grey Greet. Acid rocks, hill peat and heather dominate the higher parts of the parish, around Whit Fell at 1349 feet O.D., with glacial overflow channels well developed, especially in Black Beck.[1] Glacial drift and till (boulder clay) abound with rough benty pastures below the heather. Lower still lie the meadows and a little corn.

Prehistoric man came this way and left artefacts of flint and chert as scrapers, blades and chippings scattered across the high fields and pastures on Hewbriggs.[2] An almost perfect stone axe of Neolithic date and Lake District origin was found in a peaty field on South Dyke Farm in 1979.[3]

Similar discoveries from the district include an axe from Preston under Scar, now in the Yorkshire Museum.[4] A Bronze Age 'crouch burial' with human and animal bones and a stone axe found by a Bellerby man whilst digging drains on a rocky outcrop above Leyburn in 1957.[5] The finds are lost. Lady Alglitha's Cave on Leyburn Shawl was excavated about 1885 and produced human bones and a piece of Roman pottery.[6] Human remains were also found in Bellerby Parish, near Halfpenny House, about 1863.[7] Iron Age field systems, with earthen banks and stone foundations, abound in Wensleydale and include some on Leyburn Shawl, near Preston under Scar and at Scarth Nick top. This last has now been destroyed by quarrying. A site near Bellerby, known locally as 't'owd ruins', was recognised in 1981 as an early field system which may contain house plots.[8] Finally we note a carved stone head which was built into the front wall of an old workshop in the Wynd.[9] This, with sculpted ears, hair and

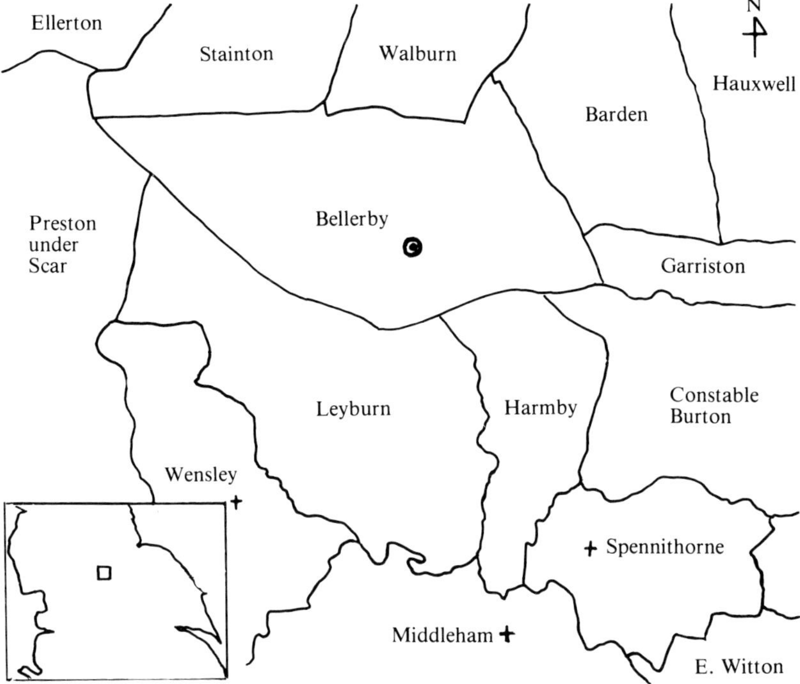

Bellerby set within a map of the surrounding townships. Bellerby, Harmby and Spennithorne made up of the ancient parish of Spennithorne where Domesday records 'Ecclesia est ibi'. Crosses mark the positions of other medieval churches in the district and the inset shows Bellerby within northern England.

a mouth hole, has been recognised as a Celtic cult object, of Iron Age date, and similar to those described by the late Sidney Jackson in West Yorkshire.[10]

Thus we see that man has lived around Bellerby for at least four thousand years. The precise date of the first settlement on the village site will never be known. Place-name evidence suggests a ninth century creation by a migrant Dane but this may be no more than a re-naming of a pre-existing farmstead. The suffix 'by' suggests occupation by people of Danish extraction about that time. It was perhaps Belg's farm but various other interpretations have been suggested.[11]

Administratively, Bellerby was a pre-conquest township and manor within the parish of Spennithorne. The present boundary remains as it was first defined for the township and the manor and their line along Abidelbek was used for the new parish of Bellerby, carved out of Spennithorne parish in 1853. The boundary marks are well documented but very few remain in position. On the map, Bellerby parish appears as a parallelogram extending south east to north west bordering onto Leyburn, Preston, Stainton, Walburn, Barden, Garriston, Constable Burton and Harmby. The village lies roughly in the centre.

The Domesday Book (1086) contains the first documentary reference to Bellerby, as for most villages. The manor then, as now, contained some 3000 acres, and a settlement with sixteen households comprising a Lord of the Manor (Enisan), thirteen villeins (unfree tenants) and two bordars (cottagers). There was land enough for six ploughs but five only were in use with eight acres of meadow. A surprisingly small amount with at least forty oxen (five teams) to winter.

Fieldwork has identified large areas of ridged ploughland around Bellerby village, all now grassed over. Could these date from Domesday? We shall probably never know but we may speculate. The Demesne lands are readily recognised on plan and by the name, Mains. They run to about 133 acres. There are about 635 acres of ridges outside the Demesne in the South Field, the High or West Field?, and the East Field? Add to this 1035 acres of rough pasture and 1200 acres of moorland and we have the known 3000 acre manor — one league long and the same wide in 1086 and taxed at £1.12.0.[12] The six Domesday carucates set against a total ploughland of 768 acres suggest a 128 acre carucate each valued at five shillings and four pence, or ½d per acre.

Those sixteen households prospered, or at least they survived, and developed their hamlet on the north row, 'ultra Lenning', above the lane as it was described in a thirteenth century charter.[13] In 1301 Edward I levied a tax to finance his war against Scotland, and at Bellerby fourteen holdings paid one fifteenth of the value of all their movable goods. The list includes Easby Abbey which paid the most for its grange at Skelton Cote, the Abbot of Rievaulx, Peter de Thorcsby, an outstanding parson of Aysgarth with interest all over Wensleydale, Thomas Hartford, then lord of the manor, John of Spennithorne, possibly the parish priest, Gregory, the shepherd and others distinguished only by their names at a time when surnames were evolving. The total amount of tax raised from Bellerby was £3.11.0. Because it was a tax levied on moveable goods rather than on land we cannot easily relate the figures to individual farms but it is interesting to see institutions emerging as the most valuable. This probably reflects land holdings as land was the principal source of all wealth at that time.

The total value of the Bellerby community then in saleable produce, livestock, grain and grass, was £53.5.0. Scottish raids, bad weather and harvest failure with consequential famine and death would reduce that figure to eleven pounds five shillings by 1334, all of fifteen years before the full horror of the Black Death hit the North.[14] If we compare the Domesday figures with those of 1301 they are remarkably similar with sixteen and fourteen households respectively. The number of households, despite vicissitudes, rose to around twenty five by 1474.

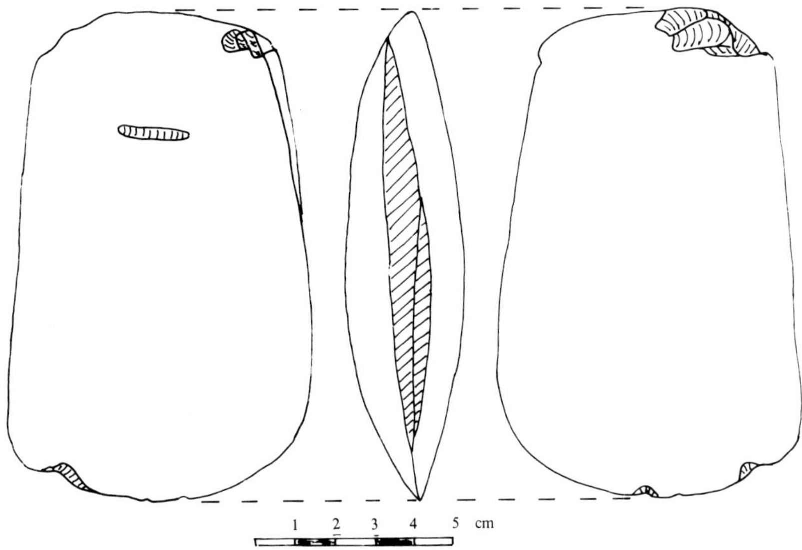

The Neolithic axe head which was found by a farmer 'stone picking' on a newly drained and ploughed field called Bellerby Ings in 1979. The axe is made of polished greenstone which can be traced back to the axe factory sites around Langdale in the Lake District.

2 Bellerby Takes Shape

Bellerby was until recently a township of many small farms and it seems that that pattern was set long ago. Great lords there were in the district and some had interests in this village but only as absentee landlords. The lordship of the manor, held by Enisan Musard, Constable of Richmond Castle in 1086, remained with the office of Constable until it was sold to the Scropes of Masham about 1330.[1]

Of more interest to us is the family residing on the manorial demesne and who were to emerge as the de Bellerbys. The first of them, of whom we have reliable evidence, is a shadowy figure called Eode, born about 1150. As documentation increases so too does our knowledge of the family. The next generation included Lawrence, Robert, Uctred and Daniele. They figure prominently in the story of this and other places in the locality as parties to or witnesses of charters concerning land transactions of the day. Elias (Helias, or Ellis in some documents) Henry and Richard de Bellerby dominate the third generation. All these men bought and sold or exchanged their lands and those of their neighbours throughout the district interminably, or so it seems from the fifty or so surviving charters.[2] Thus began the break-up of the Bellerby lands into small units.

It was Elias de Bellerby's son Thomas who severed the family's principal link with the village when, having moved over the moor to Walburn Hall in Downholme Parish, he sold out to Thomas de Hartford in 1288.[3]. The de Hartfords held Bellerby demesne for three generations and lived there before they sold it to the Scropes of Masham — henceforth in possession of the lordship and the demesne.

Thomas and Robert de Bellerby had confirmed Thomas de Helebeck's grant of Skelton Cote to Easby Abbey about 1191. The gift comprised a tenement and one carucate of land, probably about 128 acres of enclosed ground, with common rights and all within a precisely defined boundary.[4] The Abbot would give in return 'a pound of pepper at Richmond fair' annually and perform customary service, that is to undertake prescribed tasks for the Lord of the Manor.[5]

Rievaulx Abbey received several grants of land and privileges from Elias de Bellerby before 1252. They included two acres of meadow in the open fields at Bellerby, all his meadow abutting along the stream called Tervinne and the Abbey lands, and a further nine acres of meadow, in two portions, in what appears to be the West Field. To this Elias added common grazing in his pasture for four hundred and ninety sheep and thirty ewes with lambs plus the right to build shepherds' houses and sheep folds. Three more donations from Elias brought to Rievaulx a further twelve acres of meadow at Bellerby, ten and a half acres between Tervinne and Hunteresty, with one and a half acres between Tervinne and the boundary stone.[6]

Thus Rievaulx Abbey at its height seems to have held something like forty three acres of meadow and a large sheep walk at Bellerby. A messuage with twenty acres of meadow and all the common grazing passed to Sir Henry Scrope of Masham by exchange in 1315.[7] This holding might well contain all the meadows around the Tervinne and Hunteresty and lie at the core of the farm called Fryer Ings. The fate of the remaining Rievaulx lands is not known. The Scrope family were busy amassing land, power and influence all over Wensleydale in the early fourteenth century. Easby Abbey retained Skelton Cote until the Dissolution (1539) and although John Scrope secured the abbey site and much of its estate then, he did not acquire either the grange or the tenement at Skelton Cote.[8]

Ellerton Abbey, the Priory of Cistercian nuns in Swaledale, had a grant of a messuage and two bovates of land in Bellerby from Adam Preest before 1200. Precise details are lacking as all the Abbey charters were lost or destroyed during the Scots raid of 1347.[9] Coverham Abbey had property at Bellerby, two tofts and one bovate of land given by John de Spennithorne[10] and retained by the monks to 1536. St Martin's Priory near Richmond, a cell of St Mary's Abbey at York, had gifts of a toft and a croft with three acres of land and one rood of meadow from Simon Rufus de Bellerby,[11] and of one third of the tithes in the demesne from Ensian Musard.[12]

Apart from the farms called Skelton Cote and Fryer Ings, both in the north east corner of the township, we cannot identify with certainty any medieval holding. Even the two above raise questions. Several documented house plots near the main road above Skelton Cote have disappeared totally in road widening and the present farmhouse, though known to have contained wall paintings, has been heavily modernised. Nearby, on Hewbriggs pasture, a dwelling site has been found with late medieval pottery, mortar and domestic refuse. The old road or way called Hunterstye and the stream Tervinne,[13] as noticed in the charters, have not survived as land marks recognisable by those names. Huntergate, Huntergathe, or Hunterstye has to be Barden Lane from Halfpenny House to Fryer Ings and Tervinne may well be Gatelands Spring in the area once called the Tarn. Furthermore, none of the monasteries with land in Bellerby could be called, strictly, Friaries. Easby and Coverham, as Premonstrastention houses, might just qualify, but later events tend to

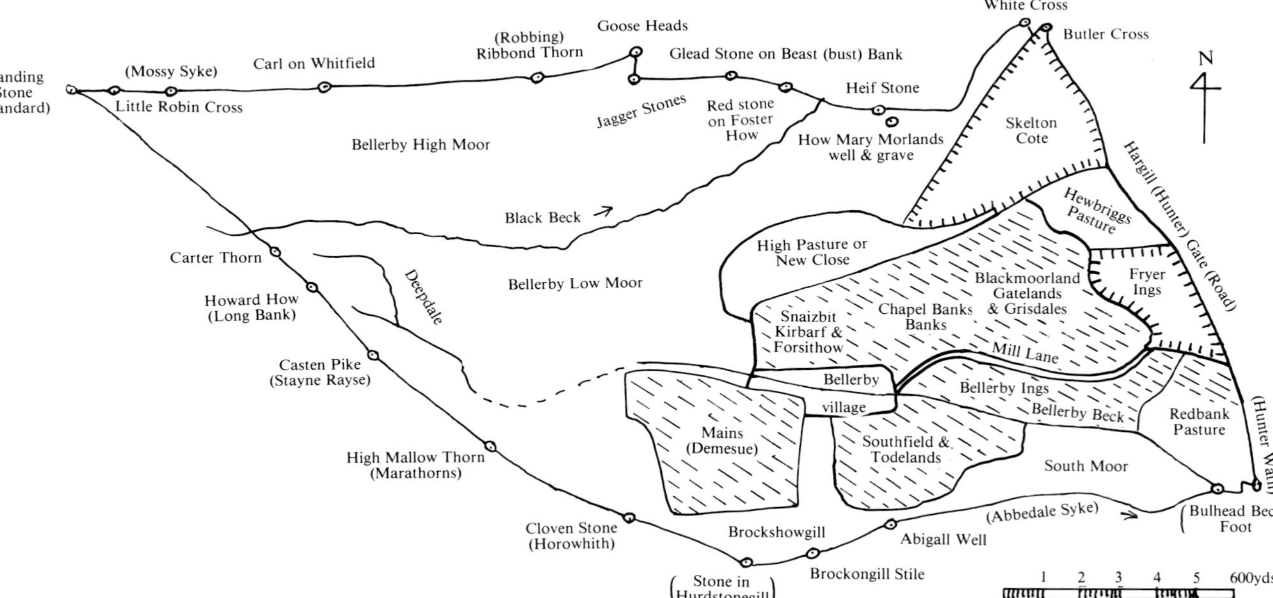

The Bellerby boundary marks based upon the enclosure map of 1773 and a boundary roll of 1863 (the latter bracketed). Hatching shows the medieaval fields, ┌┬┬┬┬┬┬┐ the bounds of separate farms from that period, with common fields, pastures and moorlands named.

associate Fryer Ings with Rievaulx and we must wonder if the name came from a family called Fryer resident there later.

The early charters describe farmland in the village as arable, meadow, pasture or common grazing and attached to tofts and crofts (house plots and long gardens, referred to in documents as messuages or tenements). The ground was measured in bovates, sometimes referred to as oxgangs, a variable area tied to quality and productivity. The Bellerby land measure has not yet been located in documents. At Caldbergh in Coverdale, a highly comparable situation, the bovate contained sixteen acres.[14] One bovate was reckoned the amount of land which could be ploughed in a year using one ox. Eight bovates made a carucate which was supposed to support a peasant family for a year. A 128 acre carucate is suggested for Bellerby, based on calculations from available evidence. The common grazing was usually directed towards the moor where a few ancient boundary marks are recorded. Prior to 1770 the moor came down to join the village green at the west end, near the Cross Tree, and extended further behind and beyond the Manor House to South Dyke and Red Bank.

We are fortunate that many ancient field names are preserved in documents and that some of them remain in use today. A distinct group recall the language of the land in such terms as rood, dale, land, rane, piece and acre, all of them words associated with arable land farmed cooperatively on strips and lynchets. Some seven hundred acres of ridged ploughlands remain, now mostly under grass. These ridges, with their distinctive curving lines, are a most impressive feature of the local landscape, especially when seen in a low winter sun from the top of Runs Bank.

No account of the breaking up of common field farming exists for Bellerby but odd survivals of the old system appear in documents; half an oxgang (1600 and 1606); a dale of meadow (1627); two pieces of ground in the town field called Gillranes (1657); and Fern Cottage with 'A Rigg' in the High Field (1683).[15] By about 1650 the open fields were becoming a thing of the past. The ground was divided up into closes, each individually owned and farmed. Some of the (then) 'new' closes clearly represent walled-in parcels of strips, while some walls or hedges cut directly across ridges of former ploughed land. Southfield remains in use as the name of a farm. Eastfield and Westfield are the names of houses but the location of former open fields of those names is a matter for conjecture.

Equally perplexing are the exact positions and extent of what look like, from the documents and field name evidence, individual common fields or blocks of strips perpetuated as named closes. These include such names as Harding, Longing, Broadleas, Snaysbit, Longacredales, Shortacredales, Chrysdales, Blackmorelands, Tackland, Toadlands ('the old lands'),

Gatelands, Gillranes, and Borwins or Borwings.[16] A document of 1320 defines three acres in Bellerby as Broadlouse, half an acre; Snaysebit, one rood; Langcresdale, three roods; Gaytesterne, one rood; Kertolfes, one rood; Estlanglyckelyt, one rood; Blackemanland, one rood; Lokensykes, one rood; Under Thyrnby, half a rood; and Bynsykes, half a rood.[17] The one field identified with certainty is Snaysebit — so called still. It lies north west of Hall Garth in the high north-west corner of the old lands within a strong cam of stone and earth with a ditch on the outside. A drystone wall makes the fence today. The original Snaysebit contained about twelve and a half acres and had ploughing strips, which remain, on four broad lynchets. Each lynchet had six ridges with prominent soil heaps marking the plough turn at the west end on the middle terrace. The strips are roughly eight hundred and fifty feet by twenty four feet, that is just under half an acre or two roods. This raises the question — would half a strip (one quarter acre) in Snaysebit be a viable proposition in 1320? How might a farmer use such a small area of land?

By the late thirteenth century, the Bellerby charters show a well established parish boundary, marked by stones, with valuable and well-used grazing within. Thomas de Hartford had confirmed his 'right and claim' on the moor from the Standard Stone through Mossy Sike and the Stainton boundary to the north and in the west via Swarthbeck (Black Beck) and the boundaries of Preston and Leyburn.[18] Robert de Hartford, similarly, had the right to graze sixty animals of all kinds, bar pigs and goats.[19] Ellis de Bellerby gave the Walburn tenants, for one penny per year per firehouse (dwelling) common of pasture 'for all manner of beasts' in Uldale (Spring Gill) 'as far as the head thereof'.[20] Meanwhile Robert de Hartford reserved common on Walburn waste within bounds thus — from Bosdale (Boston Beck) via 'Gileecuum called Bocne' to Marlemire under Hallecroft (Mary Morland's grave) then by a 'little ditch' to Gildebecks (Spring Gill Beck) and forward by the beck to Stainton.[21] Richard de Bellerby was in dispute with Abbot John of Easby in 1300 regarding the trespass, no doubt on common grazings, of Brother Walter and others of Skelton Cote.[22] We cannot define the Ox Pasture north of Black Beck as noted in 1443[23] but we may easily identify the enclosed pastures held in common as the New Close, Hewbriggs and Redbank. The South Moor was noted in 1601[24]

3 'Howseling People'

Little is known of the living conditions of Bellerby people in medieval times. Their village survives in plan only, while unrecognised fragments may remain within the structure of some houses. The homes of the middle ages were gradually replaced by longer lasting masonry buildings, on or near the old sites. Some of these 'rebuilds' survive, the oldest being the Manor House. Although undated, it was complete by 1574. The plan remains the same today as then, a row of three east-facing rooms (formerly parlour, hall and kitchen) with a buttery in a wing behind. Sixteenth century fireplaces, windows and decorative stone details are well preserved.

The prominent three-storeyed house on the high side of the green is Bellerby Old Hall. Documents do not provide a building date but architectural style and detail assign it to the seventeenth century in its present form. The fine arched fireplaces, mullioned windows, moulded doorways and some beams are clearly of that period. In the adjoining house, South View, similarly moulded beams are present, suggesting that the Old Hall once extended further east and has a more symmetrical appearance.

Bellerby has a series of highly individual doorways with wide chamfers on jambs and lintels and four-centred arches. These appear at the Old

The parlour fireplace at Corner Cottage with a four centred arch, a wide chamfer, chamfer stops, spandrels and a mason's mark.

Hall, Corner Cottage and Fern Cottage, and point to the existence of a local workshop or stone cutter in the village. They may perhaps be dated by that at Fern Cottage which was described as a 'newly built messuage or tenement house' in a deed of 1683.[1] Corner Cottage also has a good stone fireplace, with spandrels, and mullioned windows carrying mason's marks.

The seventeenth century 'Bellerby' doorway with its four-centred arch. Several examples survive in the village and may be the product of a local stone cutter or workshop.

Early features are present in many of Bellerby's houses. The farmhouse called Studdah has an ancient two-roomed plan and an early seventeenth century outshot with mullions at the back. A datestone, the oldest so far found in the village, is preserved in farmbuildings nearby. It reads M L 1674, perhaps for Matthew Lonsdale, a prominent member of the community. The porch at Hall Garth has a nicely moulded stone doorway and once had mullioned windows on the ground floor. A thatch line and an outward curve in the rear wall, for a former spiral stair, shows this to be an early house. Such a stair curve can also be seen at The Nook. Scotts Cottage has mullioned windows and at the back of Church View, the line of stones which once provided the base for a lower roof of thatch, is visible.

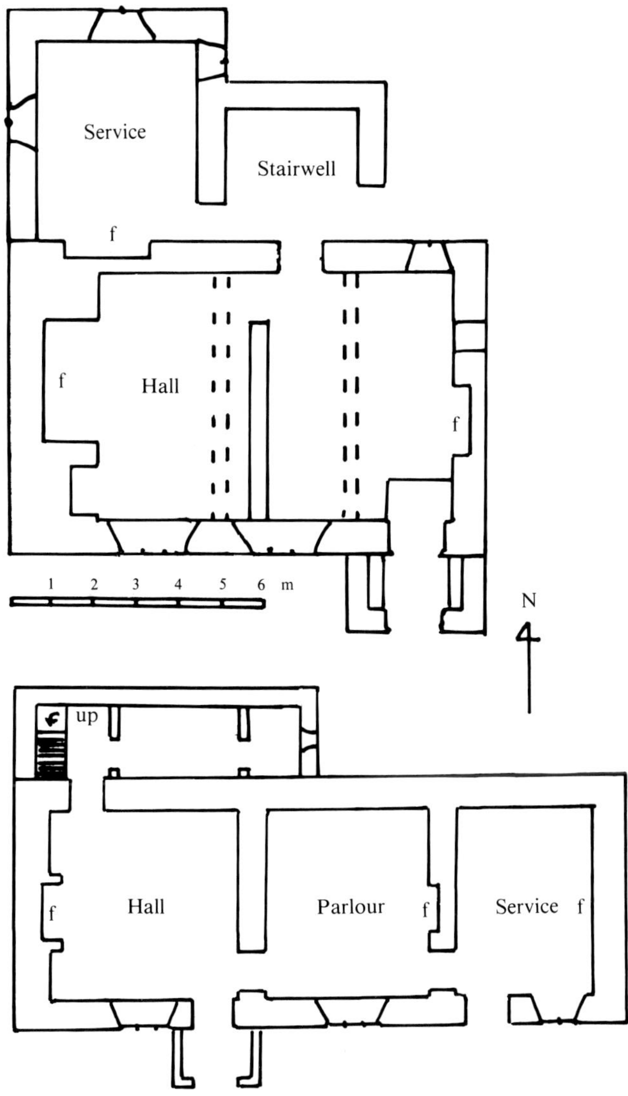

Top. The Old Hall. The surviving portion of a gentry house containing hall, cross passage, service and staircase wings. The east parlour has been identified within the adjoining house. Stone features include moulded labels, coping and finials, doorways and fireplaces. Some original woodwork survives as do decorated hinges.

Bottom. Corner Cottage. A typical 'yeoman plan' house of the seventeenth century with hall, parlour and service end, plus later additions. The house contains good stone detail in mullioned windows, a fireplace and a doorway with four centred arches, chamfer stops and mason's marks.

Several good buildings with characteristic detail, survive from the eighteenth century. The three-storeyed Old Brooke House is the most impressive, built for Richard and Phyllis March in 1732. It remains very much as they knew it except that the mullion shafts have been removed. A group of cottages at Town Head looks eighteenth century with, in the middle, an architectural extravaganza. The windows and doorway in the whitewashed front have shouldered architraves and the round windows at first floor level have similar mouldings. The kneelers at the base of the gable coping, carry carved human masks which appear older than the facade as a whole, which is c1740. Boar House has some original eighteenth century fenestration whilst that at East Grange survives complete. That house also has stylish architraves and a very handsome pediment. The nearby Hilltop also has original windows and a neat semi-circular doorhead with a keystone.

Francis and Ann Morland built a house in 1759. Their datestone is at Beckside but whether or not in its original position is open to question. Fern Cottage was wholly remodelled around mid-century. Other later eighteenth century houses include The Lilacs, Spring Cottage, the Old Post Office, and Kirkbank House. This had ochre coloured walls, iron railings and shrubs in the front garden. Church View and The Nook were both heavily modernised and the Cross Keys Inn new built after 1773. A feature noticed in the village and dating from this period is the use of brick around windows and for building chimneys on what were, predominantly, stone houses. Folk memory suggests that bricks were made in the South Field, near where The Old Vicarage now stands. Old bricks have been recovered from the site.

The nineteenth century saw the introduction of terraced rows to Bellerby in The Terrace, once known as Rowantrees. Vine House, with its vestigal fire window, is a rebuild of this period. The row west of that house, on old tofts and crofts, has interesting architectural detail in window lintels displaying flat stone arches. Pear Tree Cottage (formerly two small cottages), Brookside and Rustic Cottage, with the Shop complex and Rose Cottage have interesting details. Prospect House and Prospect Farm display high Victorian fashion but retain much older fragments and features and occupy ancient house plots

Deacon House is characteristically Edwardian, as are Eastfield House, built over older foundations, and Westfield Farm. Thistlethwaites as builders, masons and stone cutters flourished in Bellerby early this century and built at least some of these houses and for certain Aston House (1909), Bellvue Terrace, Town Head Row and Lonsdale House.

The families who inhabited the village houses over the centuries are recorded in the parish registers of births, marriages and burials of Spennithorne church. The registers give us the best view of the village families, their rise and fall over the centuries. The earliest records do not note place of residence, so we are left only with the Bellerby families known from other sources when the registers begin in 1573. John Scotte, baptized in 1582, was surely a native of Bellerby as were John Maynerd in 1592, and Thomas Haull, probably of Hall Garth, in 1607. No such obscurity surrounds William Wetherald, born near Leeds in 1589, the son of Henry Wetherald of Bellerby, 'a souldyar in Flaunders and his wife comyng to Holbecke with a pedder pack'. Fathers' names were first given in baptismal registers in 1613. Two years later, Anne the daughter of William Kendrew was christened. Such details as parson, beggar, bastard and Pucke (Peacock) occur from about 1620. North Riding Quarter Sessions ordered the inhabitants of Spennithorne and Bellerby to erect a house for Richard Peacock, his wife and children, on Bellerby waste — we presume the green, in 1656. Margaret Ianson of Bellerby was baptized in 1651 and so was Thomas the son of Thomas Hodgson from Skelton Cote. The son of Henry Fawcett, Lapidary (Quarryman or stone cutter) was baptized in 1653. Helin Blackelaund was baptized in 1670. From 1784 we are given much more detail. 1787 saw baptized Alice daughter of Henry and Ann Ridley of Bellerby; 1807 Betty daughter of William and Ann Linsley, Travelling Paupers; 1808 Richard Penhill son of John and Jane Clays of the Beacon on Penhill. The Beacon was lit as a signal during the French Wars.

The early marriage registers name the man only and include John Scotte in 1581, Thomas Hodgson 1594 and John Johnson of Masham 1610. Brides' names appear from 1613 with later that century some fathers and residences. The burial register is similarly short of detail at the beginning but the Rectorship of Francis Wyvell from 1614 improved matters. He buried Luce the daughter of William Kendrew, 8 April 1615. Anna the wife of Henry Allen, a 'Scottish Soldier' was buried at Spennithorne in 1652, adding weight to the tradition of Parliamentarians billeted in the district. James Winne and Edmond Lonsdell, both of Bellerby, died aged ninety years in 1655 and 1656.[2]

A search of Spennithorne churchyard reveals a plot of Bellerby gravestones west of the flagged footpath. Some Bellerby families, notably Pickersgill, Longstaff and Tidyman, continued to use the old churchyard after Bellerby had its own in 1847. Gravestones at Bellerby shed light on the Victorian villagers, many with familiar surnames. Clergymen, including J. H. Bleasdel and Charles White, lie here alongside Websters from the Manor House and their predecessors, the Ridleys, descended from the Osbornes. Francis Walker, the village benefactor, 'in life

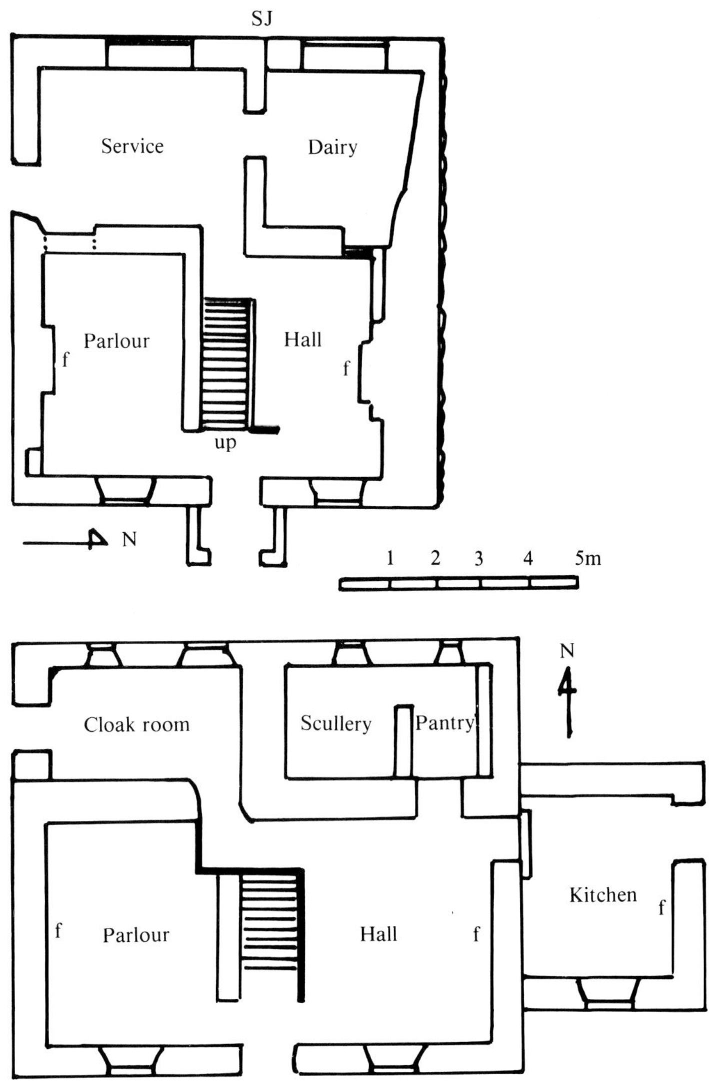

Top. Fern Cottage. A seventeenth century yeoman's house with hall and parlour to the front and a service wing behind. The dairy was added as part of a massive renovation in the eighteenth century. No early features survive, bar the service wing doorway, whilst the later work left good timber detail throughout the house in architraves, doors and hinges.

Bottom. Studdah farm. An impressive Victorian rebuild over the site of a seventeenth century dwelling. The thick back wall of that earlier house was retained with the original small service rooms beyond it. They contain early windows, one without its mullion, and evidence of a roof raising. The kitchen wing was added after the Victorian rebuild.

respected in death lamented', is buried at Bellerby as are the Brockels, father (1875) and son (1906), both called Benjamin. Some emigrants are noted and include Andrew Hodgson who died aged 22 at Hazel Green, Wisconsin, U.S.A. in 1857; Margaret Thistlethwaite who died at Hamsterley, Co. Durham, aged 25 in 1878, doubtless connected with Vicar Milner; and Herbert Thistlethwaite who was shot by the Boers in South Africa in 1902. John Gregg the besom maker is here. So too is Isabella Spence, who made the sampler at Bellerby School in 1838, and James Kendray who lived to be one hundred and one.[3]

The best views we have of how the people lived in Bellerby at various times are those from probate records for the sixteenth and seventeenth centuries. These are particularly rich in detail. One of the earliest and the best is the will of Elizabeth Symson made in 1535. Her house contained an aumbry (cupboard), kettles, a brass pot, pans, pewter dishes, a doubler, a salt and a silver horn; kists, a wooden trough, tubs, a churn, a spinning wheel and meat boards; happings (bedclothes), harden sheets and linen sheets. Elizabeth's will shows her as a woman of property and one living in some style as the items noted above formed only part of her property. Thomas Metcalfe had a rich and well stocked home at the manor in 1575. The hall, as principal living room, had tables and forms, a chair, a cupboard, a few basins, an ewer and fire irons; some cushions and two 'playing tables.' The kitchen, with a huge stone arched fireplace and beehive ovens, had brass pots, pans and ladles, etc; a cauldron, candle sticks and an apple iron; pewter doublers, trenchers, saucers and a porringer; fire irons, pans and a brass mortar; a chafing dish, scales, a cheese vat and a sinker, milk bowls, a mashing tub and a cheese trough. There were churns with staffs, sacks, a cupboard, a form, a bread grate and a folding chair. Some items had, perhaps, strayed from the buttery where there remained beer barrels, a kit and a skeel, table cloths, a harden towell, salt sellars, a little spice mortar and a bread basket. Robert Outhwaite, in 1625, had a house similarly stocked but with a stone mortar, four pairs of linen and harden sheets, linen and harden yarn, a spinning wheel and a wheel stool. There was also a little woollen yarn and a staff (probably a distaff for spinning).

Henceforth the records decline in detail and rather suggest reduced prosperity, or at least the demise of better-off residents. Ralph Blackburn's goods amounted to £1 15 0 in 1674, whereas Thomas Metcalfe had left £146. Ralph Outhwaite left £4 3 9 and Robert Outhwaite about £11. Francis Morland in 1686 had £3 10 0, Edward Favell's estate in 1696 was valued at £5 10 0. His house held a cupboard, a table and 'implements stufe' in the Forehouse; a table, a cupboard, two chairs, five pewter dishes, three candlesticks and 'implements stufe' in the New Parlour, and two standing beds and a panel chest in the high parlour. Jerome Robinson had, in 1684, a Low Parlour and a Chamber containing household goods much as in the others plus linen, harden, brass and wooden vessels. Brass and pewter remained the principal household ware throughout the seventeenth century. Christopher Dixon, shoemaker, had six pounds worth of goods in 1697 made up of cupboards, beds and bedding and a longsettle.[4]

Datestones surviving on Stephen Bell's Gatelands Farm, the property of Matthew Lonsdale in 1674, and now forming part of the milking parlour at Studdah farm. The Lonsdale inscription is cut in bold relief whereas Bell's is simply incised.

We can only estimate the size of the village community, its houses and population before 1801, the date of the first official census. The earliest recorded figure is that given in 1474 when something like one hundred people, it was claimed, lived at Bellerby.[5] Figures from the sixteenth and seventeenth century are confused by being counted as 'howseling people' (communicants) within the whole of Spennithorne parish.[6] The hearth tax of 1673 names forty-six householders suggesting a total population of about two hundred. Two thirds of the houses had a single hearth, nine had two and three had three. The remaining two dwellings were those of Mr Preston, who had married widow Crossfield from Skelton Cote, and Mr Wyvill with five and six hearth respectively.[7] The former was probably occupying the Old Hall, the latter the Manor House.

In 1789 there were around sixty houses holding about two hundred and forty people and these figures remained fairly constant into the nineteenth

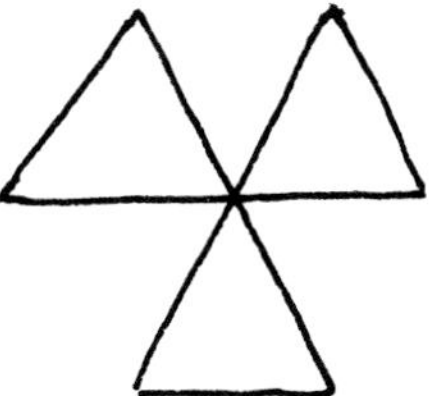

The mason's mark as found on several features at Corner Cottage, perhaps the work of Henry Fawcett 'Lapidiary', who was living and working at Bellerby in the 1650s.

century. The early decades saw a steady rise in population, described in 1811 as 'chiefly farmers',[8] to a peak in 1821 at about four hundred and ten. They occupied about one hundred and two houses giving an average family size of four. By 1841 the figures were down to three hundred and fifty people in eighty three households with twelve houses uninhabited. 1861 saw a slight recovery but decline and decay had set in. Soon Black Beck house and the Turnpike Bar fell out of use and so too did some of the village houses. By 1881 there were eleven unoccupied houses with three hundred and eleven people in seventy-seven houses.[9]

4 Fields and Farming

Francis Metcalfe, the Lord of the Manor, was heavily involved in 1602 with a reorganisation of grazing rights on the common pastures called New Close, Hewbriggs and Redbank. These, when measured and valued, were redistributed among the thirty-five freeholders and tenants of Metcalfe, Lascelles, Scrope and Butler.[1] We know from the use of the fieldname close, a newcomer to the township, and from documentary sources, that the ancient common fields were being enclosed with drystone walls and hedges about this time. By 1601 Richard Morland could sell a close containing six acres in the South Field 'in a place called Todelandes' — the old lands.[2] Some ground would remain in open fields for several decades more but by 1610 much had passed into individual ownership. We can still recognise the long sweeping lines of former ploughing strips fossilised under the present field system which is made up of groups or parts of ridges.

The early seventeenth century inventories show the farmers of the new fields to have continued much as before, to judge by their 'implements gear', with little beyond a spade, a ladder, a few hand tools and a plough with, if very fortunate, a cart. Wealth was, as is usual in an agricultural community, tied up in land, crops and livestock.

Thomas Metcalfe had grown wheat, rye, oats and barley at Bellerby Manor in 1575 whilst Anthony Outhwaite had, in May 1579, corn and hay worth thirty three shillings and fourpence. Also three acres of hard corn value three pounds. Half an acre of corn sown in 'houlacrees' was worth thirteen shillings and four pence in 1624, whilst thirty shillings worth of corn rested in the 'laith'.

Cattle appear in the inventories but in low numbers (under ten). Most farms had butter and cheese making equipment. Thomas Metcalfe had, with fifty-four 'yowes' and six rams, by far the largest holding at Bellerby in 1575. He also owned a much bigger flock and some cattle at Cotterend above Hawes. He had eight oxen, as a plough team?, at the manor with yokes, wagons, ploughs, socks and harrows. Robert Outhwaite left 'my waine & plowe with all implements thereto belonging' to his eldest son George in 1625. All the farms had horses, swine and hens, in small quantities. Likewise spades, forks, muckforks, ladders, a hay spade or an axe. Some had ling and turf for fuel.[3]

A sample of six wills dated between 1674 and 1697 shows an increase in cattle of all sorts. Small men might have a cow, a calf and a stirk, for present and future use as the milk cow. Thus had Ralph Blackburn in 1674. Christopher Dixon, in 1697, was raising a calf, three stirks and two little steers whilst Francis Morland farmed three calves, four twinters (two winters old), two stots and 'six black kine' — perhaps from Scotland. Jerome Robinson had twenty-six cattle, including ten milk cows and four oxen. Edward Favell alone had a bull among his herd of fifty-six, including fourteen milk cows.

Some had no sheep. Francis Morland in 1686 had only sixteen whereas Jerome Robinson two years previously had had one hundred and ten including, in September, thirty lambs. Edward Favell in April 1694 and Christopher Dixon in December 1697 had interesting flocks containing eighty-eight and sixty-two sheep respectively. Each had some twenty ewes and lambs and twenty wethers. Edward had twenty hogs and 'one Toope' where Christopher just had one ram.

Hay, generally in stacks, is noted as a crop with some referred to as 'course'. Jerome Robinson had, in September, twelve hay stacks with more hay in the barn and the field. Francis Morland, in September, had two stacks on the backside, and three small ones in Wildflats and the Seales. Those farmers with most livestock had perforce most horses. Robinson had seven and Favell four — each had an old mare as had Christopher Dixon. Francis Morland had 'a little small swine' — the only pig noted in this sample. Jerome Robinson had 'three waynes & one plough and gear & implements'; Christopher Dixon one cart with cart gear.[4]

These farms were all situated within the village at Bellerby but none of the present holdings, bar the manor, can be linked to a seventeenth century occupier. Two farms only, Skelton Cote and Fryer Ings, existed outside the village before 1770. Both had monastic links and the latter may well have been created by Rievaulx Abbey. Easby's grange at Skelton Cote was farmed by Christopher Wederell in 1536[5] and his descendants remained there until about 1705.[6] Should Fryer Ings lie at the core of Rievaulx's Bellerby estate then it was established as a tenement before 1300. Henry Warde was farming there in 1536 and then owed three years rent.[7] History is silent until Lady Bolton sold the farm to Richard Ellerton in 1814. His heirs, the Aldersons, sold it to David Calvert in 1891 and he rebuilt the house around 1919.[8]

Skelton Cote became Crown property in 1536 and it remained so, on off, for centuries. The Crosfield family from Westmorland leased it before 1662 and they were involved in several family disputes and lawsuits over it. The depositions tell of a forged will, rifled deed boxes, crooked agents, and Robert Crosfield giving up the premises 'having first dug up the fruit trees & done what damage he could to the gardens & dwelling house'. There

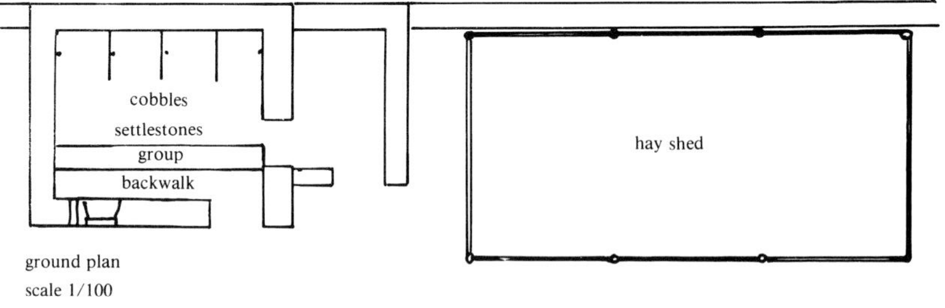

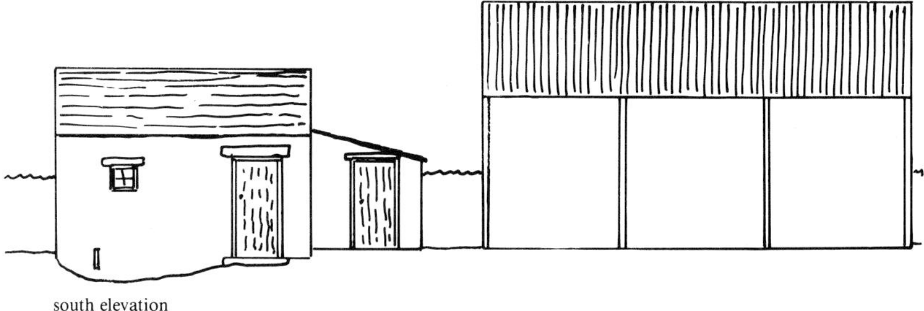

The typical dalesend country arrangement of a shed (replacing a haystack) and a stone building for housing stock. This one, called Robinsons, retains original features including cobbled stalls, stone divisions, dung channel and backwalk. A small calf-house adjoins the east end.

were at least two tenements in the hamlet up to 1774 when William Ianson secured the Crosfield's lease. The Crosfield house, in Skelton Lane, had served as Bellerby poor house with later Michael Bowes selling malt from there.[9] One Francis Nichols had managed Skelton Cote and enclosed Cote Moor in 1706-7, and William Ianson was solicitor for Bellerby enlosure award in 1770.[10]

Pre enclosure records show that Bellerby tenants and freeholders 'from time to time drove & hounded off the Wawbon [Walburn] cattle — on Bellerby Moor & very often went thither on purpose to do so & have seen Wawbon tenants...hide themselves from being seen with their cattle and used by stealth in the night to putt their cattle on'. Skelton Cote tenants had driven Walburn cattle off Cote Moor, before 1706, and when Walburn men dug turfs on the west side of Bosdale Pasture, where they had no rights, Richard Peacock and Christopher Plews, of Bellerby,... 'with a draught and cart fetched them away'. Similarly, in 1675, ling pulled by

Walburn people was removed to Bellerby and used for burning sods in the 'Whays'. Walburn men were also accused of 'graving sods' on Cote Moor. Another source of aggravation was the cutting of firewood by Walburn people in a spring (coppice) near Bosdale gate claiming that the payment of one penny per household 'smoke money' allowed this. Mr Metcalfe replied that this in fact represented the ancient fee payable for Walburn's right to graze on Bellerby Moor.

George Greason said Spring Gill represented an old stinted pasture, one looked after by a herdsman called Foster, and that Foster How took its name from him — 'from his blowing his horne on the hill top in the morning'. George Wright of Bellerby used to 'staffheard' Bellerby moor about 1685 and he often dogged Walburn stock back across the boundary. He also claimed that William Ridley of Bosdale bribed him with promises of money, christmas cheese, meat and drink, to allow him onto the moor but he refused all.[11]

The 1770s saw the end of any kind of common pasture farming with the enclosure of the three pastures and the moor. An Act was secured in 1770, commissioners appointed and public meetings held to explain procedure and take in landowners' claims. The ground was measured, valued and distributed according to the old stint. The resulting scene remains with us today. All had been walled in or enclosed by hedges within a few years., Tithe disappeared as a church due at this time as Bellerby Chapel and the Rector of Spennithorne were in receipt of valuable allotments, mostly near the Turnpike.[12] Several new farms were created at Red Bank, Hobthrush — known as White House before it was dismantled in 1960, and Black Beck, above the deer park and long since abandoned to ruin. The farmhouse at South Dyke was built in the 1920s on fields belonging to Prospect House.

Late eighteenth century agricultural improvement brought soil science to Bellerby in the form of burnt limestone as a dressing for acid land. Two men were engaged to pare fifteen acres of Bellerby common, at 12/6 an acre, in 1776. Four limekilns, called running kilns, were built in the Deer Park, at Chapter Bottom, on the Mains and one, for public use, in the Moor Road quarry.[13] These stone built kilns, mostly round, were filled from the top with a mixture of limestone and fuel which when burnt ran out at the drawing arch as lime. The kiln ran for several days. The tenant at the manor was allowed the use of quarries and kilns in the Deer Park and the Mains in October, November and December each year.[14]

These years saw the foldyard with open fronted shelter sheds for cattle developing and several were built at Bellerby. One stands at the top of Hewbriggs built around a laithe; one much altered stands in the South

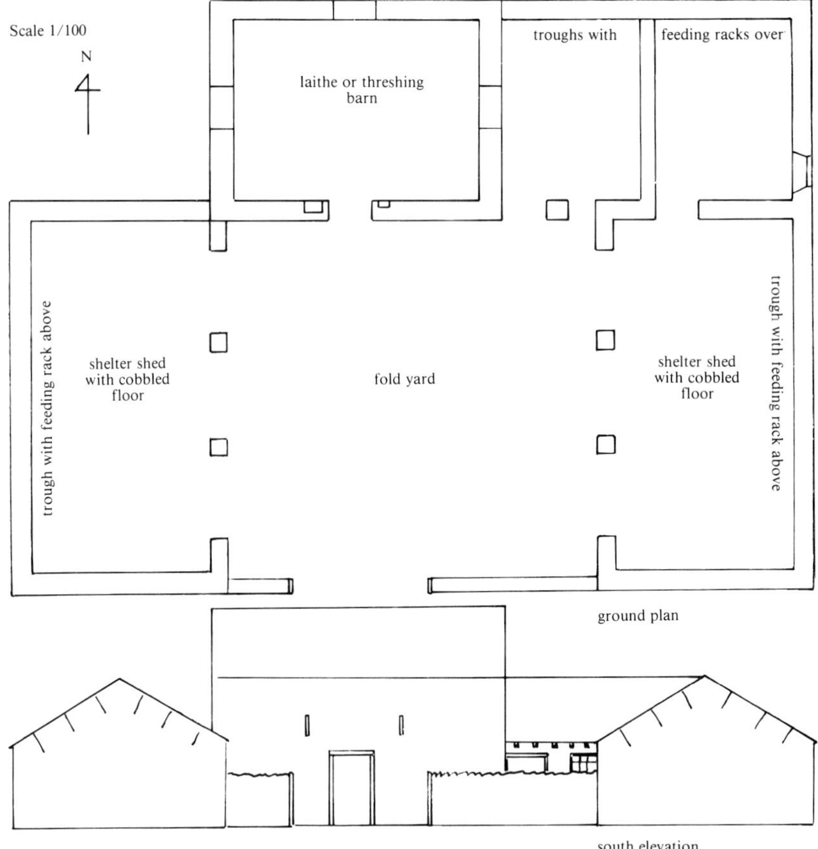

The foldyard with shelter sheds built around a pre-existing laithe or threshing barn on Hewbriggs. The laithe had a doorway on each wall, presumably to take advantage of the wind whatever its direction. The sheds were built of stone with brick dressings, king posts roofs and superior fittings. Roofing material is grey flag throughout.

Field; a third was built in the enclosure numbered Seventy One. The old pattern of a small stone building for cattle with a stack or a shed remained, and remains, in use across the old fields. The farm buildings at the Manor and at Southfield were all rebuilt, the latter to incorporate a horse gin in a wheelhouse.

When, in 1789, Matthew Brown took a sixteen year lease of the two Spennithorne Rectory allotments near the moor road the landlord agreed to build a barn, stable and fold garth as directed by Mr Gill of Constable Burton. These remain. Matthew might burn limestone for the land, take two crops only of hay or straw each year to be consumed on site leaving manure. He must keep and maintain a dog for the Rector, likewise graze his horse for three months each year without payment. He would, after eleven years, lay down to grass 'in a good husband like manner', fourteen acres in the lower allotment and sow with clover and grass seeds chosen by Mr Gill.[15]

The new tenant, John Dent, at the 'High Farm under Whitfield', probably Bellerby Moor, was allowed the use of the Low kiln 'to burn lime for what he wants to lay upon the Grounds' when the landlord was not using it. Meanwhile Mr Chaytor, as landlord, would make tenable the

COW CLOSE FARM, NEAR LEYBURN.

TO BE SOLD BY AUCTION,

BY MR. RICHARD HOLMES,

On MONDAY, the 1st day of NOVEMBER, 1858,

ALL the STOCK of Cattle, Sheep, Horses, Corn, Hay, Turnips, Eatage, Implements of Husbandry, &c., the property of the late Mr. William Dobson, deceased, consisting of 8 Steers, two years old, forward in condition; 4 Steers, three years old, forward in condition; 4 fat Heifers, 2 milk Cows, 6 fat Sheep, 17 good-bred Lambs, 15 three-parts-bred Lambs, 20 half-bred Ditto, 1 grey draught Horse, aged; 1 ditto Ditto, rising four years old, by Grey Coverdale; 1 grey Horse, rising five years old, by John Bull, dam by President; 4 fold-yard Pigs. 14 stacks of Oats (2 black), 2 stacks of well-won Hay, 1 stack of Clover, 9 acres of Swede and white Turnips, 8 acres of over-eaten Fog, until the 25th of March, 1859, and 19 acres of Pasture Eatage until the same time.

The IMPLEMENTS comprise 1 long Cart, 1 coop Cart, with broad wheels and shelvings complete; 1 Ditto narrow wheels, with shelvings; 2 iron Ploughs with wheels (by Busby), 1 wood Ditto, 2 Turnip-cutters, 1 large Roller, 1 pair of Harrows, double Turnip Drill and Roller, 4 Ladders, 1 stand Heck, 1 sheep Rack on wheels, 1 Scuffler, 1 greasing Stool, 1 corn Rake, 1 corn Crusher, 1 Sweep, 1 Corn-bin, Stack-bars, Rakes, Forks, Shovels, Gripes, water Tubs, pig Troughs, pig Tubs, and Gearing for 3 horses complete.

Also, a quantity of HOUSEHOLD FURNITURE.

The whole of the Straw, Hay, and Turnips to be taken off the premises, except "Toadlands" Turnips, which are to be eaten on.

Credit will be given on approved security for the Corn, Hay, Turnips, and Eatage until the 25th March, 1859, or 5 per cent. allowed for ready money.

The purchasers of the Corn will have the use of the Barn, Thrashing and Winnowing Machines.

The Auctioneer particularly requests an early attendance on account of the numerous lots and the shortness of the days.

The Sale to commence at Eleven o'clock precisely.

Leyburn, October 19th, 1858.

A very detailed advertisement for the sale of William Dobson's live and dead stock at Cow Close Farm, near Bellerby. Published in the *Ripon and Richmond Chronicle*, 30th October, 1858.

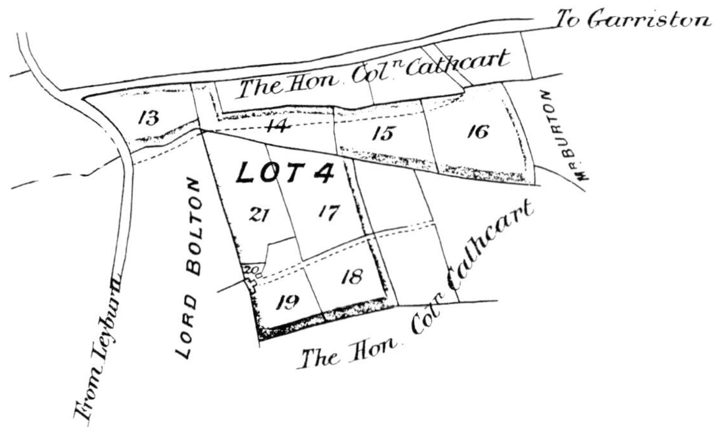

Lot 4.

All that HOUSE and OUTBUILDINGS,

situate in the Township of Harmby, known as Cow Close House, together with several Closes of Arable Meadow and Pasture Land, situate in Bellerby and Harmby aforesaid, containing in the whole 39a. 1r. 30p. or thereabouts, now in the occupation of Mr. Richard Wade.

SUMMARY OF LOT 4.

No. on Plan A.	Description.	Cultivation.	Quantity. A.	R.	P.
13	High Abergail	Meadow	4	1	30
14	Low Abergail	Meadow	4	2	15
15	South Lands	Meadow	4	2	8
16	South Lands	Pasture	6	1	3
17	Cow Close	Meadow	6	1	29
18	Cow Close	Arable	4	1	37
19	Cow Close	Meadow	3	1	8
20	Cow Close, House, and Outbuildings	——	0	0	35
21	Cow Close	Arable	5	0	25
		Total	39	1	30

Plan and sale particulars of Cow Close Farm as sold by public auction at Leyburn, 19th June, 1891. Richard Wade's holding was smaller than that William Dobson had in 1858 when he occupied the fields called 'Toadlands' as part of Cow Close.

house, barn and 'Helmn' and build a cow house if John Dent would lead the stones. Hedges were to be repaired and replanted as necessary. The farm comprised pasture, meadow and arable for which a detailed rotation was planned between 1795 and 1798. This was to include rape or turnips, oats and seeds.[16] The new lessee at the Manor in 1855 might pare, burn, plough or rive up land for tillage at a price; and grow white corn, pulse, clover, collseed, turnips or green crops provided they were not sold off; fodder crops were to be consumed on the premises and well decomposed manure and bones might be imported. The weather as usual had the last word. A note from Bellerby reported the last sheaf carried home on Thursday night, 28th October, 1858, and that a shower of snow fell next morning.[17]

After 1850 some Bellerby farmers were among the leading stock breeders and practical innovators in the district. Mr Stewart had for sale, after three years at the Manor, twenty-two Ayrshire calving cows and heifers 'selected from the best breeding stocks, consequently of a quality not often seen here.' He also maintained a flock of Leicester, Cheviot and half-bred sheep.[18] Advertisements in the local press show how farmers might improve their blood lines. The Autons of Bellerby had a stallion, called Farmers Friend, which would attend and cover mares for one pound at Bedale, Northallerton, Richmond, Leyburn and Reeth. He was a rich brown bay, clear of white, black legs and standing sixteen hands with great power, fine symmetry and good action. His pedigree included the best cart horse in Lincolnshire. Farmers Friend was claimed 'to be the fastest cart horse in England'. William Brown, also of Bellerby, maintained a stud boar, bred by J. Proctor, which would serve sows at four shillings each, 'pre paid'.[19]

Barden's first agricultural show in 1860 saw Robert Stirk, Stewart's successor at the Manor, doing well with geldings and fillies along with his neighbour William Wardell. Stirk was at East Witton show whilst Wardell and Rev J. G. Milner were at Catterick Horse Show. 'Honest' John Osborne's horse Bellerby, ridden by Lee, won the Coverdale Steeplechase in January 1867. James Hodgson took first prize at Leyburn Market Club show for cottager's best sample vegetables. The Vicar, Rev Milner, took poultry to both Richmondshire (held at Leyburn) and Northallerton shows.[20]

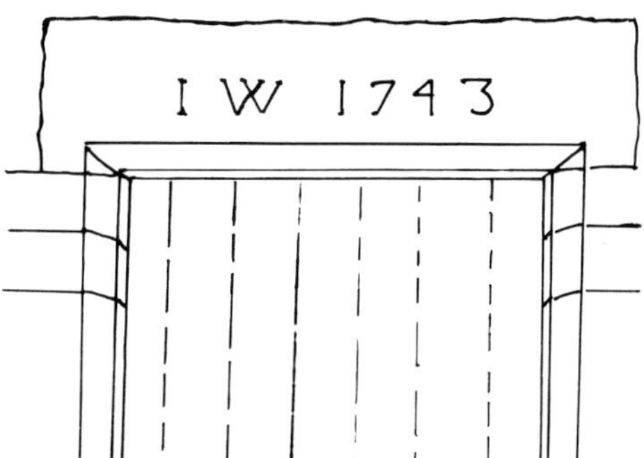

Dated and initialled doorhead on a very fine stone-built barn near South Dyke. It stands in that part of Bellerby 'South Field called Todelands', the old lands. The builder has not been identified.

5 Some Lords—

By 1330 Bellerby lordship and demesne belonged to Sir Geoffrey Scrope and his son Henry, who did not live in the village, but were based at Clifton Castle near Masham.[1] Whilst the Scropes owned Bellerby they or their appointees held sway over everybody and everything through the manor court. Sir Geoffrey was a leading lawyer, a diplomatist, a judge and chief Justice of the King's Bench. He died in France but was brought back for burial at Coverham Abbey.[2] Bellerby remained with his family until 1415 when the third baron, Sir Henry, was executed and his estates forefeit for involvement in a plot to overthrow the king. Bellerby passed to the Crown. Thus affairs of state touched the most remote village.

A Scrope cousin, Henry Lord Fitz Hugh of Ravensworth, had a crown grant of Bellerby and many other manors, soon after the execution.[3] The Fitz Hughs, perhaps Richmondshire's most ancient and illustrious family, held vast estates in the district and beyond and looked to Jervaulx Abbey as their spiritual home. Manor Court rolls survive, though incomplete, 1442-1863, and afford rare glimpses into village life. The court was styled Court Leet, Court Baron and View of Frankpledge, roughly translating as Justice, Land, Search and Arrest. The officers, Steward and Bailiff, were joined later by Pinder and Bylawman.

The Steward, sometimes given as Seneschall, sat with a jury drawn from the free tenants. Rents and fines were collected with fines for non appearance. More recently by-laws were drafted and enforced, boundaries ridden and gamekeepers appointed.[4]

A mid fourteenth century list of tenants included, among others, Robert Spark, William Whitby, John and Thomas Plewes, John and William Pratt, Adam Tirry, William Hogeson, Robert Sympson, Reginald and John Outhwayt, John and Christopher Wilson, Thomas Darwent, Reginald Dobson, Robert, Thomas and William Scrafton, Thomas Siggiswick, John Cowper, Edmund Lonesdall, John Raby and William Sowerby.[5]

A court roll of Lady Alesia Fitz Hugh, dated 1497, notices old and newly arrived family names in the village. One person was fined a shilling for illegally grazing sheep on the common pasture whilst five men and a woman, Issabell Prat, were prosecuted for insufficiently winnowing in the South Field. Eight were fined for having an inadequate fence against the common and Christopher Scrafton was particularly concerned with the common pasture called 'Hubrigelessa.' The corn mill, as a manorial

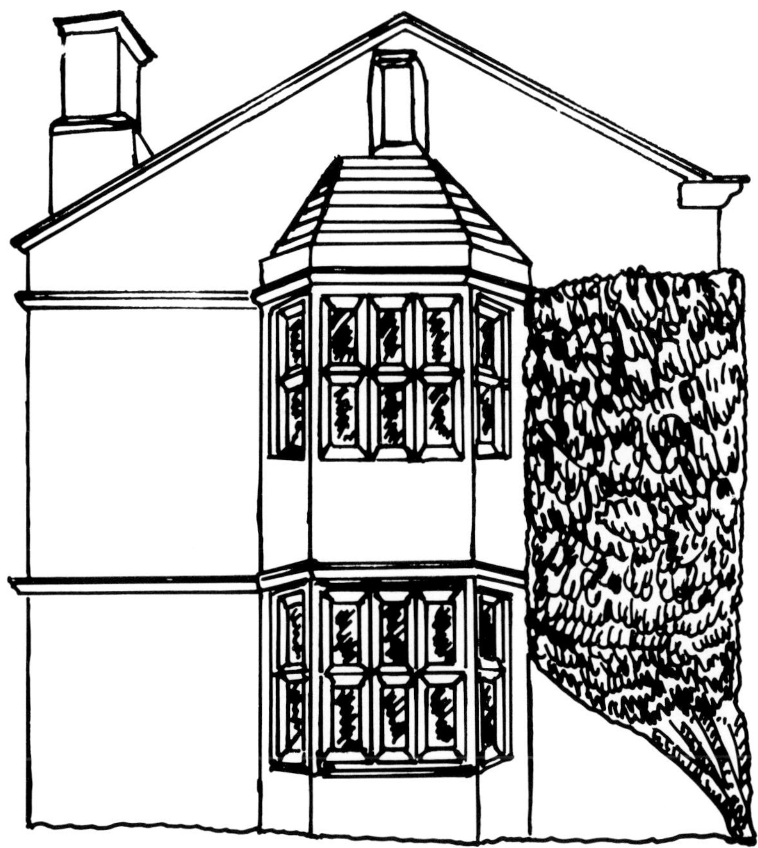

Bellerby Manor House showing the south gable complete with sixteenth century mullioned and transomed windows in a stone-built bay, moulded string courses, gable coping and chimney stack.

perquisite with a monopoly of grinding, belonged to Fitz Hugh. It appears that the tenants were responsible collectively for its 'blades' which were exceedingly defective as was the 'watter whele Axiltre' — so given in English in a latin document.[6]

The Prior of Coverham and the Prioress of Ellerton were noted among the free tenants in 1511. So too were John, Gerome (?) and Robert Symson of a family well established in Bellerby by the sixteenth century. In 1535, during the troubled times of the Reformation, Elizabeth Symson, widow, died. Her will tells of provision made for her sons, of her clothes and personal possessions and of her charity, also her household furnishings (described elsewhere). Firstly, the welfare of her soul is considered. It is committed to the care of God, Saint Mary and all the Saints. Four pence is bequeathed to Spennithorne high altar, sixpence to the priest, and fourpence to the Grey Friars at Richmond. She wishes her son Christopher to be educated, so 'he canne write and rede', and she leaves money for this purpose.

Family heirlooms include a silver horn, and garments. Elizabeth's 'best sleves' (separate and often elaborate items throughout the Tudor period), caps, kerchiefs and kirtles to female relatives and even to Agnes 'Rament made for her of old Raymentes.' In a household of considerable style and comfort, good fabric was not to be wasted. Simon, the eldest son, was to have the farm, the cart 'and all that belongs yt', Christopher and Agnes could have all the residual goods 'to helpe them' whilst every house in Bellerby had 1d.[7]

The reign of the Fitz Hughs and their heirs ended about 1570 when the Metcalfes bought the manor. This branch of the family from Nappa Hall in Wensleydale came to Bellerby via Bear Park near Aysgarth, London and Bedale. They were sometimes resident but as London lawyers they were often living there or elsewhere. The first, Luke Metcalfe, of whom we know little, and his wife Katherine Jackson, came from Bedale.[8] Their son Thomas owned and farmed Bellerby manor farm to his death in 1575.[9] It passed from him to his brothers Nicholas, then Mark the Vicar of Northallerton and finally Matthew. His son Francis had it next[10] but left it in the hands of minions.

The break up of the village lands into smaller units continued. Richard Peacock, husbandman, bought his farm in 1562. So too did the yeoman James Outhwaite who also purchased half his father's holding. Elizabeth Simpson had half a messuage for herself well before 1600.[11] A brief survey of the Metcalfe lands made by Matthew in 1594 shows twenty-four tenements attached to the manor. Precise details are not recorded but the document agrees substantially with those given in the stinting agreement of 1602.[12]

The interdependence of landlord and tenant is well illustrated in the lease whereby Francis Metcalfe of Louth in Lincolnshire let portions of two tenements and three oxgangs of land at Bellerby to Thomas Walker in 1606. Thomas was to pay a rent of six shillings and three pence, at Pentecost and Saint Martin's, with two fat hens at Christmas. He was also to fetch and deliver by cart three quarters of coal, paying the pit price, to the 'sometime dwelling house of the lessor in Bellerby'. He must grind all his corn at Bellerby mill and plant each year four trees of oak, ash or elm 'which shall best agree with the soil'. Also lead stone to make six roods of wall and 'perform six bowne days work when called in haytime and harvest'.[13]

The Metcalfe's retained Bellerby through at least seven generations and extended their land holding whenever or wherever possible. Their boundary ridings and boundary disputes generate some of the most colourful and informative records we possess. Thomas Metcalfe rode the bounds in 1665 and, according to a witness, Thomas Wright, 'gave out silk points (laces) and nipped them by the ears and bid them remember'. Dr Adrian Metcalfe led one hundred people round in 1685, and demolished an un-sanctioned new fence in the Rough Close.

Stephen and Leonard Robinson were Stewards, referred to archaically as Seneschall through these years as they pursued the Metcalfe's jealously guarded rights. They led ridings in 1705 and 1715 but details have not been recorded so perhaps there were no confrontations. The area most at risk from encroachment was that covered by the former Easby Abbey lands where some of the boundary marks agree with those discussed above.

By 1725 John Metcalfe was locked in a legal dispute with Sir Roger Beckwith of Walburn over the boundary between Skelton Cote and Boston Farm in Walburn manor. Metcalfe claimed a line from the Butler Cross (lost in road widening) near Halfpenny House, west by the hill top to Marlemire, through the Rough Close and White Myres to the Heif Stone near Bosdale (Boston) Gate. William Ridley had broken up the Heif Stone to build up Bosdale Gate in 1714. Coaches and carts previously used that way as the main road to Richmond. The line ran west to Busty Bank, beyond Uludale (Spring Gill) to the Rubbing or Ribbond Thorn.

Beckwith sought a boundary from the Butler Cross by the lane to Skelton Cote taking in some of that holdings lands, definitely in Bellerby Manor. He continued across the Rough Close, as enclosed in 1586, south of Mary Morlands Grave by the Long Rigg and the Green Way to the Parsons Staggarth. Beckwith said that his grandfather was killed early in the civil war and that his father was then spirited away to France and lost until 1660. Meanwhile, he claimed, the Walburn estate was in total confusion, with the house garrisoned by 'Captain Sutton and officers in the Parliament service', and the Metcalfes taking advantage on the boundary. The Walburn claim was built around an ancient grant of grazing rights supposedly issued by William de Bellerby.

The place known as Mary Morlands grave, and its position on or off the boundary, was crucial in resolving the disputed line. We know nothing of poor Mary Morland but that she 'hanged herself' in Bellerby about 1690, was denied burial in consecrated ground as a suicide and was therefore buried on the moor. George Wright 'knows the place where Mary Morland was buryed which is within the Lordshipp of Bellerby who about 35 years since hanged herself. It was concluded she should be buryed at Whitemyer near the corner of the Rough Close between two Lords [Lordships], but the Bier whereon her body was born broke and her body being nausous buryed her on Bellerby Moor near Long Rigg end and [G.W.] was the first that opened the ground for her grave where she now lyeth'. George Jones, who helped to carry her said 'she was intended to be buryed nigh the corner of Rough Close but the stey or bier breaking in the way she stank and thinking no harm they buryed her where the stey broke... they carried hack and spade along with them to make the grave'. Thomasin Swales, niece of the deceased woman, said that the ladder upon which the body was being carried broke forty yards short of the boundary, near Richmond Road, and Mary Morland was buried where she fell on Whitemyer, near the corner of Rough Close and Long Rigg. One Margaret Hop, aged seventy-five years in 1725, saw the men go out of the town with the body. There were no women with them. Thus, though the grave was mentioned as a boundary mark, and one deeply rooted in the folk memory of the village, it was not in fact on the boundary.[14]

A less dramatic but no less interesting inquiry concerning the moorland boundary took place in the summer of 1770 whilst the enclosure award was being prepared. This concerned Mr Simon Scroope of Danby, his rights in Stainton Lordship, and the boundary west of the Carl of Whitfield (Whitfell), through Moses (Mossy) Syke to the point called Standing Stone and Little Robin Cross west of the Grinton Road, The enclosure commissioners rode the boundary on May 8th, drafted their plan, and had an objection from Mr Scroope on July 19th. Depositions containing much valuable information were compiled subsequently.

One Christopher Metcalfe recalled how, forty-five years previously Mr Scroope had been asked 'leave' to get turf south of Moses Syke and that Bellerby men never got turf or ling on that ground 'but it was by way of stealth'. He remembered that Mr Scoope gave two loads of turf and they got three 'and that they stuck fast with a load upon that ground'. Mr Scroope, being nearby shooting, sent a strong mare and helped them out. Edward Bowes of Bellerby, it was recalled, got ling and turf south of Moses Syke and it was carried away to Stainton. Also that Matthew Dent led away the ling that was pulled by Francis Morland. Turf and ling were, we assume, to be used as fuel and roofing materials.

A thin seam of coal lay under the heather at this point and workings known as Scroopes Pits were situated south of Moses Syke. The boundary then had strong financial implications. James Hudson, Lee and Partners, coal miners, had mined coal on Stainton Moor in 1754. Mr Scroope claimed that John Raw and Matthew Dent 'drew water at the shaft I sunk in the year (1754) & both of them were paid by Rich. Summers my agent at that time'.

He also said that the boundary mark called Rubbing Thorn 'is ribing thorne' which used formerly to be hung with ribbons 'when the boundary were road', and that Harry Stephenson's father planted it and gives this information.

Simon Scroope and John Metcalfe settled the matter together, on the moor by walking backwards and forwards across the heather with a post until a mutually satisfactory spot for the boundary could be agreed.[15]

6 And Men

The eighteenth century opens in Bellerby with a note of charity. The great lords had withdrawn, lesser gentry remained and the community was beginning to regulate itself. In 1711 Christopher Dixon made a will leaving a rent charge of five pounds a year at Christmas, derived from the fields called West End Town Gartley, Gartley and Snasbitts. The Overseer distributed the moncy among those in the village less well off and not in receipt of poor relief. The rent had declined to five shillings by 1832 since when the charity has disappeared altogether.[1]

Francis Walker, a resident landowner, gave the interest off £300 in 1874 to provide coals for the poor at Christmas, an idea derived perhaps from Christopher Dixon. He also left investment interest to the National School, the Vicar and the Wesleyan Methodist Minister. The coal charity survives but its value has declined so much that distribution happens irregularly.[2]

The spirit of independence led the freeholders and inhabitants into open dispute with the Lord of the Manor over the use of Bellerby Chapel. They engaged Mr Crosfield, of Skelton Cote and Middleham, to draft Articles of Agreement and an Affidavit to defend their right to attend divines service at the chapel. This, they claimed, was 'late seized with force and violence' by John Metcalfe. They said that when Ellerton Abbey had lands in the village the monks erected a small religious house and a chapel to which the Abbey appointed a Priest at four pounds a year paid from the said lands. The estate had fallen to the Crown at the Dissolution, was sold to Neville, and the four pounds reserved. This information was supposedly derived from the books of Gale, Ecton, Burton, Drake, and others. Those works do not in fact support the inhabitants' claims.

The Freeholders continue thus — 'there is at this time (c1725) a very antique altar table of stone...in the chansel...which is separated from the body of the chaple with very antique workmanship in wood and a chaple bell at the west end'. The walls were thick, the windows and doorway all 'mitred' and the chapel garth looked like a burial ground being filled with earth dug from outside the walls. The inhabitants had from 'time immemorial' repaired the chapel by church assessments and always appointed a chapel warden. The Abbey ground, called 'Chaple Lands' where foundations of an old religious house remained in 1725, were in the hands of John Metcalfe whose ancestors had paid the four pounds to the Rector. At Easter twelve months previously John Metcalfe had taken possession of the church by fixing an iron bar across the door and by

Bellerby in 1856 from the first edition Ordnance Survey map drawn at six inches to the mile. Note the pinfold, smithy, The Boar P.H., the corn mill, and the smallness of the school building. Copy from NYCRO.

posting guards with arms thus preventing entry by the reader and the people. This, they claimed, caused them great distress, the village being 'a great distance' from any other church. The situation was also a great 'encouragement of vice and immorality'.

The freeholders had sought and had advice from the Solicitor General who suggested that they demand possession and payment and that if those were refused then send the affidavit to the Court of King's Bench. John Metcalfe flatly refused to comply thus the freeholders agreed to follow that course paying all Mr Crossfield's charges and expences. The outcome is not known, the evidence is highly questionable, the antique fittings, if they were present in 1725 have not survived, but the fact that the inhabitants were prepared to fight for their rights clearly demonstrates their attitude as a community.[3]

A handful of manor court records have survived from the century between 1760 and 1860, years during which the court as an institution became increasingly anachronistic and powerless. It was concerned principally with by-laws governing the common pastures up to 1770 and thereafter with the village green, the roadside verges, encroachment on the waste, public nuisances and the watercourses.

John Metcalfe was Lord of the Manor in 1760, John Yarker the Steward, Francis Lonsdale the Bailiff who was empowered to levy fines by distress — that is by taking goods in lieu of cash. Most fines were levied for encroachment: ie, building a stable, a pighull (pigsty), a porch and stairs. James March had made a courtyard before his dwelling house and Richard March had built a wall which turned the water out of its ancient channel. Some seventy-three freeholders were named and thirteen jurymen were chosen from their number in 1764. William Walker and Henry Favill were sworn in as Bylawmen.[4]

The by-laws drafted in 1764 give a rare insight into township government for that was the role the manor court was assuming at this period. The principal work was the regulation of the common pastures. Dates were agreed for opening and closing the commons, the stint was settled (the number of animals allowed on), and the amount of fencing, draining and shepherding to be undertaken during the year. The town streets were protected from the dumping of dung and carrion. Unrung pigs and unbowed geese were not to wander at large in the township. Bowed geese had a leather thong placed round a wing joint to prevent flight. Besom makers who damaged hedgerows in search of besom shafts would be punished. Those who burned bracken on the moor and sold the ashes, presumably to soap boilers, attracted the most hefty fine.

Residents were not to encourage vagabonds, travellers or tramps etc to linger in the town more than one night lest they become a charge on the poor rates. The streams and watercourses, especially the mill stream called the High Beck, were to be properly scoured out and the footbridges kept in proper repair so that silt did not accumulate and flood the town.[5]

John Metcalfe appointed gamekeepers from 1725 to 1766 when Henry Brotherton of Harmby had the post.[6] That year saw the sporting rights throughout the grounds, commons and wastes leased for nine years, at six guineas a year to Sir Marmaduke Asty Wyvill of Constable Burton. The sport was deemed to include killing and destroying game of all kinds bar conies.[7]

Metcalfe ended his family's interest in Bellerby when he sold the Manor, the Lordship, the Advowson and certain farms and allotments to William Chaytor of Spennithorne in February 1774.[8] This branch of the Chaytors were rising in local esteem and they, though resident at Spennithorne, were near and able to take a lead in the life of the village. Theirs, it appears, was a generous paternalistic and philanthropic attitude towards the chapelry and township for eighty years. The church, church life and the community benefitted much from their generosity.

It was, perhaps, early in the Chaytor era that the foreman of the jury in the manor court drafted a set of proposals aimed at relieving the poor and the poor rates. It suggested that the lanes and wastes of Bellerby, hitherto occupied by people of property, might henceforth be used by the poor alone. That is those owning one cow or one horse might have free liberty for them but pay for summering any extra. The proceeds from such lettings to be given to the Overseer and the Foreman of the Jury for distribution at Christmas to those too poor to own any animals. The poor's geese, but no more than two plus a gander and goslings, would have free access. The Foreman would issue directives which must be obeyed e.g. only quiet animals would be allowed on the waste and lanes. The 'Poor People' are those 'deemed not to be worth forty pounds, and who really belong to the township of Bellerby'. The stock of others found in the lanes 'not attended or watched Day and Night', would be impounded.[9]

By-laws drafted in 1789 show an increasing awareness of good agricultural practice in that 'we present and amerce [fine] every person who shall turn any horses, mares, sheep, or other cattle infected with the scab, or any other infectious decease upon the wastes or into the highways and lanes within this manor, for every horse, mare, sheep or beast...£1.19.11.' The by-laws concerning pigs and geese were reiterated; there were drainage problems on Hubrigs Lane and William Frier the Miller was in trouble over the mill race. This court met at Joseph Pickersgill's house, an inn, with John Breare as Steward acting for William Chaytor.[10]

Christopher Topham had taken over as Steward by 1809 presiding at two meetings. The first a formal declaration of business, the second to draft by-laws and deal with encroachment by banning or charging an extra rent. The by-laws continued much as before with the inclusion of Tups (Rams) and Riggots (half castrated rams) not allowed on the commons and wastes between October and February. The fine was five shillings.

Encroachments were noted at Cross Head, Townhead Quarry, Runs Lane and on the Turnpike verge. John Walker had 'erected shops' on the waste, Christopher Bushby 'a small shop', others had made a garden, a pighouse — to be pulled down forthwith as a nuisance and 'detrimental to the water and the public'. Steps into a granary remained, so too did Francis Raw's flower garden. Where and why so many shops? we ask. It appears that there was money in the town for building plus a need to cultivate every inch of ground and inspiration to grow flowers.[11]

The court had returned to the Manor House by 1819 with James Willis as Steward. John Airey was Pinder that year and in 1820. The by-laws continued, so too did encroachment but less extensively. George Emerson was Bailiff in 1820, Richard Pattison in 1824 whilst Airey continued as Pinder. There were that year fifty-three freeholders and sixty-seven tenants and occupiers. Edward Plant had taken in twelve perches of land at 'Ewbridges' for which he must pay a stiff fine or remove his fence. Meanwhile Edmond Lonsdale, having built a goose house, six yards square, on Mains Lane might keep it upon payment of one penny per year.[12]

The last recorded manor court was that held on 30 April, 1863 with Thomas Topham as Steward for John Osborne. Seventy-five tenants and occupiers were listed and William Thistlethwaite was sworn in as Pinder. Much of the business was set form — the by-laws drafted concerning scab, tups in autumn and winter, bulls and stallions barred from the commons, pigs and geese could no longer roam 'at large'. Impounded stock might be released upon payment of sixpence or fourpence. The mention of a double stint on the moor suggests that some common grazing survived the enclosure award on Whit Fell.

The court fined those found wilfully soiling the water supply or turning it out of its course; those piling stones, manure, and rubbish on the town streets, wastes and highways. James Hodgson and William Roantree were fined each of them one shilling for leaving dunghills beside the road whilst occupiers of houses near the beck were similarly fined for allowing stones and rubbish to remain and interfere with the waters. The Surveyor complained of a private householder's bridge which 'being too narrow and limited prevents the free flowing...of the beck' and injured the high road. Elsewhere the Surveyor was required to remove or break up stones and rubbish on the highways.[13] By 1890 the scene was set for the creation of a new scheme of local government. There is no record of a parish meeting in the village but, elsewhere, a parish council came into being in 1894.

John Howe Osborne, of Brecongill, Coverdale, Training Groom, purchased Bellerby Manor, the Lordship, the Advowson, the Manor House and several farms from Chaytor in 1854. He rode his bounds on the day of the court in 1863. Osborne never lived at Bellerby but one of his daughters, Jane, and her husband, James Ridley, farmed Southfield and Bellerby Manor at various times. Their descendants remain in the village today. 'Honest John' Osborne, the Jockey, inherited Bellerby from his father in 1867[14] and ran a horse called Bellerby at local sporting events.[15] The Osborne heirs retained the estate for a hundred years and parted with it in portions. The Manor Farm was sold to Raymond Scott, the present owner in 1954.[16] A pasture near Skelton Cote and the Advowson of

Bellerby Church remain with an Osborne heir. A silver plate and stained glass window in the church recall the family's connection with the village.[17]

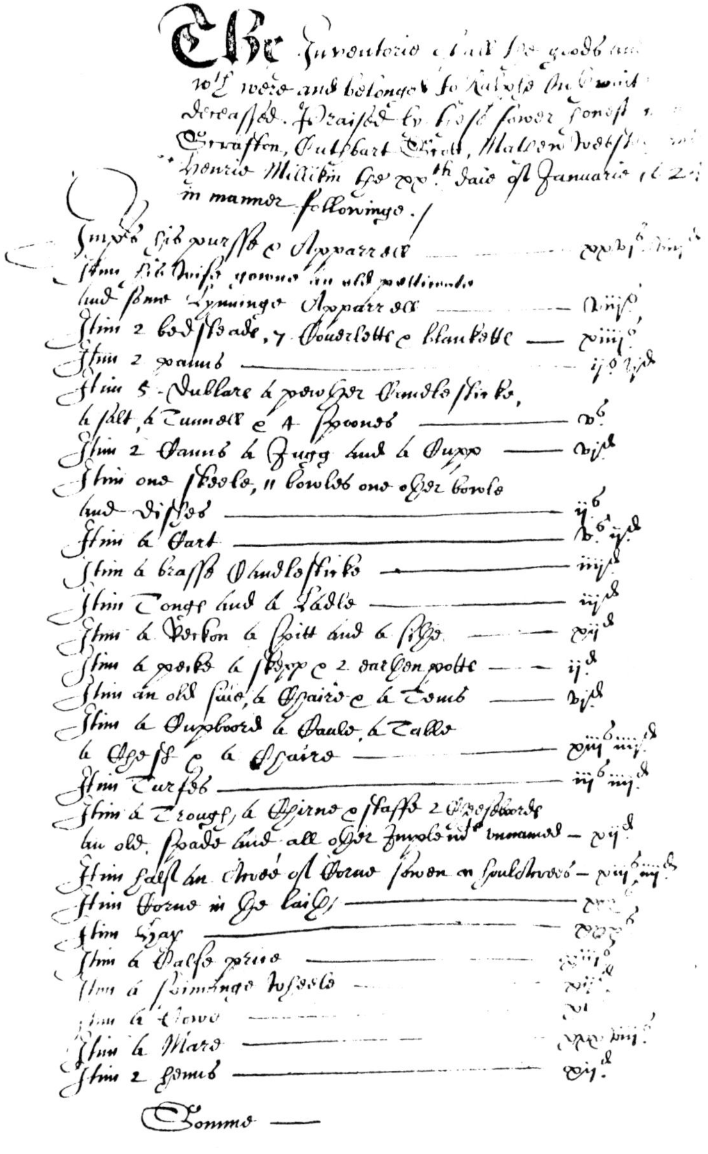

The Inventorie of all the goods and [illegible] which were and belonged to Raphe Outhwait deceased. Praised by these fower men [illegible] Grafton, Cuthbert [illegible], Mathew [illegible] and Henrie Millikin the xx th daie of Januarie 1624 in manner followinge./

Imprimis his purse & Apparrell — xxvj s viij d
Item his wifes gowne an old pettiecote and some lyninge Apparrell — liiij s
Item 2 bedsteads, 7 coverletts & blanketts — viij s
Item 2 pannes — ij s vj d
Item 5 dublers a pewther candlesticke, a salt, a tunnell & 4 spoones — x s
Item 2 cannes a Jugg and a cuppe — vj d
Item one skeele, 11 bowles one other bowle and dishes — ij s
Item a Cart — v s ij d
Item a brasse candlesticke — iiij d
Item Tongs and a Ladle — iij d
Item a [illegible] a spitt and a [illegible] — xij d
Item a [illegible] a [illegible] & 2 [illegible] — ij d
Item an old [illegible], a chaire & a combe — vj d
Item a cupboord a [illegible], a table a chest & a chaire — xiij s iiij d
Item Turfes — iij s iiij d
Item a trough, a churne [illegible] 2 [illegible] boards an old [illegible] and all other [illegible] unnamed — xij d
Item halfe an acre of corne sowen on [illegible] — viij s iiij d
Item Corne in the laithe — xx s
Item Hay — xx s
Item a calfe price — [illegible]
Item a spinninge wheele — xij d
Item a cowe — [illegible]
Item a Mare — xx s viij d
Item 2 hennes — xij d

Somme —

Raphe Outhwait's probate inventory, 20 January, 1624. LCLA.

7 St John's Church

The church of St John at Bellerby was built in 1874 but that was only one chapter in the long story of religious activity in the village. Written records take us back to the fifteenth century but the beginnings are obscure and remote linked with the foundation of Spennithorne parish and church. This parish began as a long narrow strip of land with Spennithorne church at the bottom, near the river Ure opposite to Middleham, and Bellerby at the top under Whit Fell on the Swaledale boundary. Three separate townships made up the parish as Bellerby, Harmby and Spennithorne, with medieval chapels at Harmby and Bellerby.[1]

Successive Lords of the Manor appear to have maintained private chaplains at Bellerby, a common enough practice, but one that may well lie at the root of later confusion when the earliest chapels are considered. An undated land grant made in favour of Coverham Abbey mentions Samson the Clerk but the best of our early references come from the family of de Bellerby who, as principal tenants of the demesne from at least 1150, held sway in local affairs. Elias de Bellerby had by 1236 given the parson of Spennithorne a house and land at Bellerby in return for the right to maintain a private chaplain at his own cost. John de Bellerby, Clerk, had a gift of ground next to his house in 1281 and was probably the man referred to as John the Clerk de Bellerby, a notable member of the community until at least 1307. Thomas de Bellerby was master of the Knights Templars Preceptory on Penhill in 1309 and we wonder if he was the Thomas who parted with Bellerby demesne in 1288. Certainly he was excommunicated, later absolved, for wearing the Templars' habit after prohibition. John Lorimer of Bellerby, Chaplain, sold his inheritance there to Sir Henry Scrope in 1372.[2]

William, Lord Fitz Hugh of Ravensworth had the manor from 1442 and subsequently held a court baron. Complaints were laid there, almost at once, against the Rector of Spennithorne for not celebrating mass at the 'chapel of St Oswald' at Bellerby. Henceforth, for thirty years, the charge was repeated and recorded on the court roll until the people finally lost patience and sent their complaint to the Pope. The foundation of this chapel, like that of its contemporary or successor, St Catherine's, is lost but it is likely that one or both grew out of a private chapel. The dedication was not mentioned in 1474 in the petition to the Pope begging him to 'sponsor' the use of Bellerby chapel for mass and to have the Rector of Spennithorne appoint a priest to occupy the house already there. The

The silver chalice given to Bellerby's new Chapel by Miss Jane Chaytor in 1802. Jane was the daughter of William Chaytor, Lord of the Manor and Patron of the Chapel at the time of the rebuilding.

population, with that of Skelton Cote, numbered more than one hundred and they were frequently denied access to the mother church because of flooding at Abidelbeck. The Archbishop of York was instructed to investigate but the outcome is not known. The case is not noted in the Archbishop's register.[3]

Chantry Certificates from 1546 mention the incumbent of Spennithorne parish and 'one other pryst...at the finding of the parson', who together ministered to two hundred and twenty 'howseling people'. The second man was in all probability stationed at Bellerby. One John Awbrey and others had a Crown grant in 1586. This included 'a chapel with curtilage, founded for the maintenance of a priest to celebrate mass in... Bellerby, in the tenure of Charles Lonsdale. A close, called Le Chappell Close, three acres of arable land, in Bellerby, given for the maintenance of a priest in the chapel of Bellerby'. The Lord of the Manor, Francis Metcalfe, in 1601, let to Richard Firbanke of Aldbrough a 'Chappell with the Chappell Garthe...called...St Katherines Chappell' with waste and common at

Bellerby. Thereafter the chapel and its garth are lost but folk memory points to a site near the foot of Runs Bank where the fields, called Chapel Bank and Kirkbarf, reinforce that belief. In September 1814 there was let to George Bainbridge 'the stones...from the Old Chapel. 2.0.0.'[4]

Spennithorne parish registers record the people of Bellerby using the mother church for baptism, marriage and burial from at least 1573. The Rector had had his way and they came to his church for formalities at least — those, that is, who were not drawn to the old faith or later to nonconformity. Thomas Crosfield, Rector of Spennithorne 1649 - 1663, a scholarly man, kept his register in latin, and left us a very detailed terrier of glebe lands in Bellerby Town. They included a tithe barn with a little Parrocke, Dodsons flatt, Parsons flatt, Borwins close with Dicke pasture or Wildlees alias Wythdikes, altogether about ten acres plus common rights.[5]

1723 saw Bishop Gastrell of Chester, in whose Diocese the Archdeaconry of Richmond then lay, mount a Visitation. This found Bellerby two miles from the parish church and John Metcalfe of Gray's Inn, Lord of the Manor, paying a 'Lay man' four pounds a year to read prayers and a homily every Sunday forenoon and afternoon. We must presume a chapel of sorts be it St Oswald, St Catherine, or another. The records give no hint of venue. The eighteenth century was a weak period in the Anglican church almost everywhere with absentee incumbents and neglected buildings. Bellerby people continued to use Spennithorne for rites of passage but the enclosure map of Bellerby, made in 1773, shows a chapel on the site occupied by St John's in the middle of a 'Chapel Yard'. The enclosure award of 1772 set aside certain allotments, two on the moor and one beside the chapel yard, and called Chapel Green, for the benefit of the Chapel. That building, whatever its status or dedication, was demolished in 1801. It was described from memory in 1874 as being 'nothing short of an out office'.[6]

We have no name for the lay man noticed in 1723 and we know of no other cleric, bar the Rector of Spennithorne who was also Curate of Bellerby, until 22 April 1775 when the Rev John Hogarth was appointed Perpetual Curate at Bellerby, 'this turn by lapse'. A draft commission to license was issued by Archdeacon Blackburn of Richmond, and Hogarth, in true eighteenth century fashion, was absent living at Newcastle. The Visitation for 1789 shows the chapel in a very ruinous state with no clergy house, even though there had been one earlier, and the living in receipt of four lots of Queen Anne's Bounty. John Hogarth died in 1802 and was succeeded by the Rev James Tate, MA, master of Richmond Grammar School and holder of several other livings in the district. He was at Bellerby

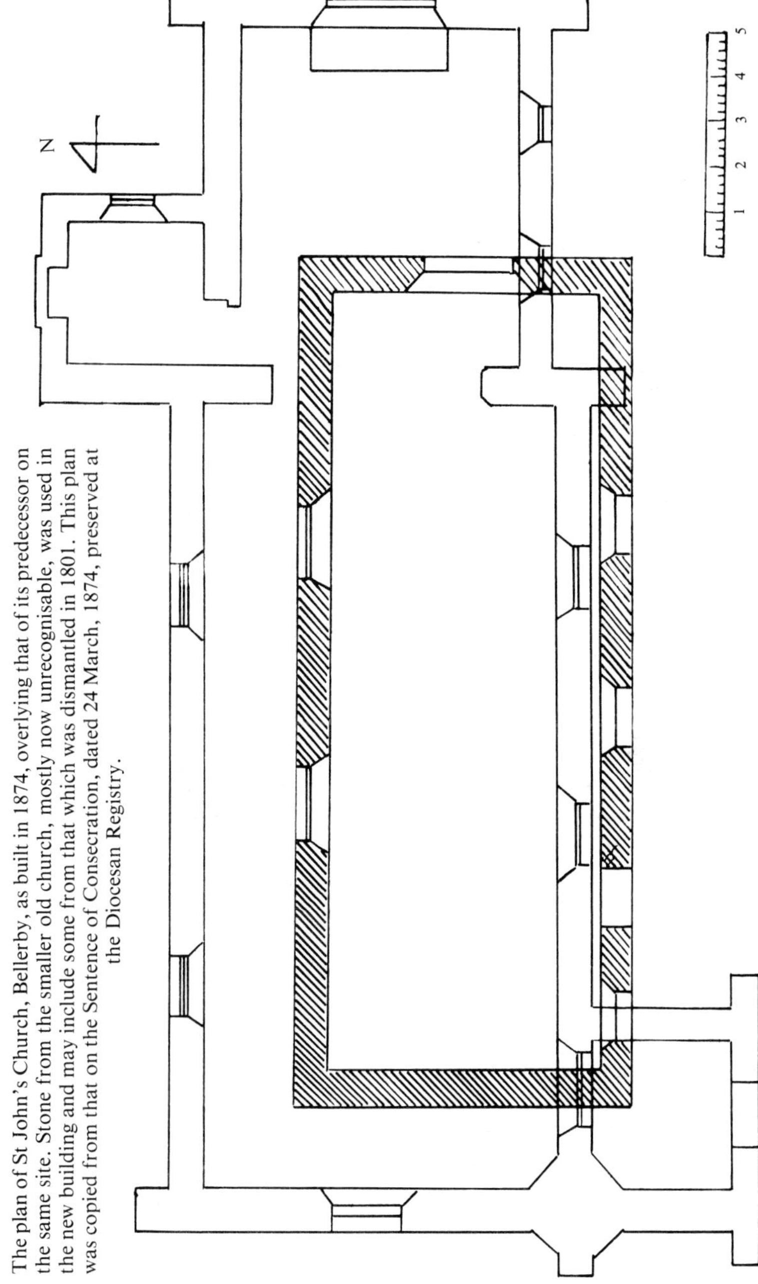

The plan of St John's Church, Bellerby, as built in 1874, overlying that of its predecessor on the same site. Stone from the smaller old church, mostly now unrecognisable, was used in the new building and may include some from that which was dismantled in 1801. This plan was copied from that on the Sentence of Consecration, dated 24 March, 1874, preserved at the Diocesan Registry.

The Choir at St John's, Bellerby, c1954.

Front row left to right: Kathleen Sayer, Irene Mawer, Ken Sayer, Richard Walker, Trevor Tupling, Eric Bainbridge, Robin French, Murial Gregg. Back row left to right: Fred Walker the Churchwarden, Alfred Hindle, Rev Robert Simpson the Curate, Mrs Dorothy Walker, Mrs Murial Sayer, George Horner, Margaret French, George Ride, Mrs Mary Clarke, Raymond Scott, Fred Pearson.

on Good Friday 1803, but left most of the work to the officiating curate, William Kirkbank. Tate resigned in 1808 and was followed by the Rev Francis Blackburn, Rector of Croscombe Wells in Somerset where he was resident.[7]

The Officiating Curate throughout was the Rev William Kirkbank, 1752-1842, whose sixty-seven years at Bellerby make him the most notable of all the village clergy. He came of a family long settled at Whicham, Cumberland. His ordination as Deacon took place at St George's, Bloomsbury, 8 April 1776, on which day he received the curacy of Millom. He had begun at Bellerby the previous year, under John Hogarth, and was noticed in the Visitation of 1789, resident and in receipt of twenty-six pounds a year. By 1794 he had thirty-five pounds when he had due to him fifty-four, representing two thirds of the living.[8]

Kirkbank House, overlooking the village green, is said to have been his home and the Visitation of 1825 has him living one hundred and twenty-five yards from the chapel. He was very active throughout the first two decades of the nineteenth century and was often at Spennithorne church. Bellerby remained unlicensed and minus a burial ground. William made his last entry in the parish register in 1832 and seems then to have retired, aged eighty. He lived on another ten years, died and was buried at Spennithorne 15 September 1842, aged 90 years. A large box tomb marks the spot. His niece and companion, Miss Elizabeth Kirkbank, remained in the village, a notable personality in 1844. A second niece, Nancy Kirkbank, married the Rev. J. G. Milner who was Curate and Vicar at Bellerby for fifty-six years and his son, the Rev. William Kirkbank Milner, Rector of Knarsdale, near Alston, took a funeral at Bellerby in October 1870.[9]

Bellerby Chapel was rebuilt in 1801 as a long monotonous building resembling a stable with a bell-cote and few windows. We have no fuller description than that. The patron, William Chaytor, who bought out the Metcalfes in 1774, was probably involved but left no mark, unlike F. J. who carved his name and the date 1801 on a kneeler which is preserved. A delightful double handled silver cup made by John Longlands of Newcastle, marked 1770, and inscribed J.C. came to the chapel at this time 'The Gift of Miss Chaytor To the Chapel of Bellerby 1802.'

The rebuilding seems to have aroused old aspirations and an acid memorandum in 1805 in Spennithorne register complains that Bellerby people 'wish to separate themselves from the Mother Church'. But progress was slow. Nothing happened until July 1847 when C.W.C. Chaytor sold the chapel yard for use as a burial ground and it was consecrated by the Bishop of Ripon 2 August 1847. The chapel was also licensed for baptism and marriage but the erection of 'The Chapelry

District of Bellerby' north of the 'Abbergill brook' did not appear in the London Gazette until May 1848. A rash of large decorated headstones celebrate the spirit of independence and it was only a matter of time before full parochial status was sought and won, in 1853.[10]

Assistant curates began to appear at Bellerby about the time that William Kirkbank gave up but we know very little about them. Robert Colebank was there in 1833; William Heslop, BA of Queens College, Cambridge came in 1835; and Alfred Gatty, BA, served 1837-1839. He was something of a scholar with political and literary connections, the product of Eton and Oxford. He found Bellerby chapel so small that 'the trombone player near the door had to raise his projecting instrument to let the congregation pass under'. Gatty lodged alone at Leyburn, walked each Sunday to Bellerby, had lunch, which comprised two biscuits and a new-laid egg, with the parish clerk, then took the service. He hated his cure and would have left but his Bishop forced him to stay the two years. He settled later at Ecclesfield and stayed there as Vicar for sixty-three years. J. W. Boyde was curate in 1841, with later that year M. G. Boydell. Richard Ellis came next, in 1844, and we know more about him because he was active, vocal and had connections. His name crops up frequently in the *Wensleydale Advertiser*. He stayed about two years and was succeeded by William Cumby, BA. He was a local man, from Middleton Tyas, a twenty-five year old bachelor who lodged with a farmer, John Greathead. He stayed until 1853 and saw the chapel licensed, the churchyard consecrated 'and the funds for building the vicarage raised'.[11]

Francis Blackburn's long term as Perpetual Curate ended and James George Milner took over in 1829. He was born at Bolton on Swale in 1796, Ordained at Chester and Licensed to West Witton in October 1823, the year in which he married Nancy Kirkbank. He was Perpetual Curate of Hamsterly and died there 16 March 1885. Fragmentary records suggest that he resided in Bellerby from the building of the new Parsonage about 1853 for around twenty years. The later years of his term saw the church served by Edmond Casey to 1879, Thomas Robinson to 1882, and J. H. Phillips to 1885. Henceforth the Perpetual Curate, styled Vicar from 1868, was constantly resident and a curate seldom employed.[12]

Moves towards a major restoration of the chapel were afoot in 1861 when a note appeared in the local paper decrying the plainess of the building and its lack of beauty whilst striving not to upset the church-wardens by hinting at neglect. Bellerby, it claimed, was 'almost destitute' of wealthy inhabitants, thus subscriptions were being sought from owners of land there who lived elsewhere, so that the work might proceed as soon as possible.[13]

John H. Osborne and Francis Walker brought the scheme to fruition in 1873 - 74. Mr J. Jones of Leyburn, a native of Bellerby, was engaged as architect and contractor and he chose to build in an Early English style. The old chapel was demolished completely and a larger one built on the site. Old stone was augmented with new from Half-penny House quarry, which provided stone for a large octagonal font. Varnished pine seating for two hundred people was installed, also two stained glass windows.

The new building was consecrated by the Bishop of Ripon 24 March 1874, 'to be and remain a Church by the Name of the Church of Saint John at Bellerby for ever'. Proceedings began at 11.00 a.m. with the Bishop met at the church door by the curate, the Rev Edmond Casey, and the Churchwardens, James Ridley and Robert Stirk. About a dozen surpliced clergy were present with a congregation of three hundred plus Leyburn choir to lead the singing. Lunch was served in the schoolroom for clergy, gentry, choir, churchwardens etc. The whole venture cost about six hundred pounds, raised wholly by subscription, the result 'a comfortable and pretty church'.[14]

Space prohibits a full account of the life of St John's but its place in the community became dear and remains secure. Its priests have served it well and two in particular are well remembered. James H. Bleasdell took up the cure in 1886 and died at Bellerby, much lamented, five years later. Likewise Charles A. White, Vicar for twenty-seven years from 1918. Both were deeply involved with the village at large, the former as school correspondent and remembered by the pupils as 'a grand man'. The latter in a public spirited fashion in reviving the sword dance and operating as air raid warden when almost blind. Their spirit lives on.[15]

Bellerby church was rebuilt in 1801 and in 1874. A stone kneeler from the former is preserved in the front wall of the latter. F. J. was probably a churchwarden or a stone mason but the name is not recorded.

Perpetual Curates and Vicars of Bellerby

1775 - 1802	John Hogarth
1802 - 1808	James Tate
1809 - 1829	Francis Blackburn
1829 - 1885	James George Milner
1886 - 1892	James Hamilton Bleasdell
1892 - 1902	Horace Rimington
1903 - 1904	S. Ross
1905 - 1917	H. W. Heighway
1918 - 1945	Charles A. White
1946 - 1950	Eric W. Lawson
1953 - 1955	V. A. FitzHugh
1956 - 1968	Charles Clifford Peake
1968 - 1972	Thomas Foster Unsworth
1973 - 1981	Geoffrey N. R. Sowerby
1981 - 1988	David Johnson
1988	James Mellors

Officiating Curates

1775 - 1832	William Kirkbank
1833	Robert Colebank
1835 -	William Heslop
1837 - 1839	Alfred Gatty
1841	J. W. Boyde
1841	M. George Boydell
1844 - 1845	Richard Elllis
1845 - 1853	William Cumby
1873 - 1879	Edmond Casey
1879 - 1882	Thomas Robinson
1883 - 1885	J. H. Phillips
1953 - 1955	R. Simpson

8 Catholics and Nonconformists

Bellerby has always had a few people who were faithful to the old religion, inspired perhaps, by the local Catholic families such as Scrope at Danby, Waite in Leyburn, Thoresby of Barden, Wyvill of Spennithorne and the Metcalfes from Bear Park — the direct ancestors of the family at Bellerby Manor. Some at least of the Catholic houses had secret rooms or priest holes. James Waite is recorded a Jesuit c1640 and his family, and their heirs the Thornboroughs maintained a private chapel at Leyburn. A note of 1713 has forty persons present at mass there — in the house of Mr Shephard, perhaps the tenant. The estate passed to the Riddells in 1774 and the chapel was registered at Quarter Sessions in 1791. A Catholic Church was built at Leyburn in 1835.[1]

Meanwhile the Scropes had built a mass house at Ulshaw, four miles from Bellerby, in 1788 at the core of the present house and chapel there.[2] This concentration on gentry families is misleading in that lesser men are overlooked. The wealthy alone were worth pursuing and prosecuting unlike the poorer denizens of Bellerby who were left alone and missed out of the records.

They emerge later in the eighteenth century in replies made to the Bishop's visitations. By 1789 William Kirkbank could report only one Catholic family in the chapelry, by 1804 four families were present and

The Bellerby Methodists built their chapel in 1839 and marked the event with a neatly carved stone tablet. The building survives, the oldest chapel in use in the Wensleydale Circuit.

remained in 1811. He claimed 'No Papists' in 1814 but that is difficult to reconcile with what went before and came after. In 1821 they were 'not many — stationery in numbers', but at 1825 he was back with three families[3] — all very confusing and doubtless a source of grave concern to the Curate who saw the Methodists progressing. Henceforth, so far as we can ascertain, there would always be a few families and individuals attached to the Catholic faith in the town.

Richmondshire was an important centre for Quakers in the seventeenth century, especially around Richmond and Hawes. Leyburn developed as something of a minor centre with a meeting registered in 1689 but in an unidentified private house, probably that of Matthew Hutchinson or James Ianson.[4] There never was a purpose built Friends Meeting House at Leyburn.

Ralph Ainsley, the blacksmith and whitesmith of Bellerby, was the leading Quaker in the district and had meetings at his house. One such was broken up on 13 May 1660 when at least thirteen Friends were hauled out and abused by 'armed men' with swords, pistols, guns, staves and stones. Men and women were beaten till blood was shed, several were knocked down and bruised. Those from Richmond and Marrick were followed onto the moor where they were beaten again and some 'punched' until 'some were for some time senseless'.[5]

Ralph Ainsley stuck to his faith and suffered financial loss by it. He was fined by distrainment, for meeting, and lost pewter worth about sixteen shillings in 1671, two cows, a mare, two stacks of hay and 'a burden of hay off his wife's head', together with three burden ropes and two hay spades 'by which it appears they will leave little'.[6] Ralph died in 1676 and left his wife Jane a house, smiddy, two garths and a field called Baddack. He was worth thirteen pounds representing two cows and a mare, bellows and implements of trade, household goods, a cart and a hay stack.[7] He was buried in his own ground at Bellerby with others of his family.

Quakerism in Bellerby survived but only just. There was never a proper meeting house. The nearest were at Richmond, Aysgarth and Masham. One family alone survived from 1789 to 1811. By 1814 that had gone and the sect seems never to have been revived in the village.[8]

The preacher evangelist, Nicholas Manners, came to Wensleydale in 1765 at the behest of Christopher Simpson of Redmire who had heard John Wesley at Leeds a short time before. Nicholas arrived at Bellerby, his first stop, on horseback, and addressed an open air meeting on the green. The natives were not impressed, indeed, they were distinctly hostile and 'they drove him out of the village as if he had been a highwayman'.[9] He went on to greater things further up the dale whilst Bellerby languished, though

A Blaſt blown out of the North, and Ecchoing Up Towards the South, to meet the Cry of their Oppreſſed Brethren.

A brief Relation of ſome of the Sufferings of ſome of the Lord's People in Scorn called Quakers, *at and near* Bellerby *in the* North Riding *of the County of* YORK, *the 13th Day of the 3d Moneth, in the Year* 1660.

UPon the ſaid day ſeveral of the ſaid people from ſeveral parts in and about *Richmond*, *Maſſam*, *Coverdale*, and ſome other of the adjacent Places, being met together at the Houſe of *Ralph Ainſley* in *Bellerby* aforeſaid, to wait upon and worſhip the Lord, two men came and called *Ralph Ainſley*, and told him, *They had Order to break up the Meeting*; but before Friends in the Houſe had any notice (for *Ralph* then being buſie ſetting up Horſes had not told them) there came divers Armed Men Ruſhing to the Door, crying, *Where are theſe Rogues? We have Order to break up your Meeting*; ſome of them ſaying, *We will cut you as ſmall as Bread.* Whereupon one of thoſe People ſo met, went to the Door to underſtand the Real Cauſe of their ſo coming, and whether they had any Order to hinder the ſaid peaceable Meeting, or they in their own Will had taken in hand to do it; who in Meekneſs ſpoke to them and told them, *That they were there met*

in

The opening paragraphs of Richard Robinson's account of the breaking up of a Quaker meeting at Ralph Ainsley's house in Bellerby, 13th May, 1660. Copied from the book, *A Blast blown out of the North,* published in 1680, and now at the North Yorkshire County Library.

not for long. By 1789 William Kirkbank had to report to visitation some few Methodists 'but none of any rank [they] seem rather to decrease' and had no meeting house. He gave virtually the same reply in 1804 but by 1811 he had given up and reported only that they had no 'dissenting place of worship'.[10] In 1824, the date of the first recorded preaching services in the village they were being held fortnightly, at 7 p.m., and led by local 'exhorters'.[11]

By then, or soon after, a Society was formed with Mr Walker, its first member, 'who entertained the Preachers for years'. By 1828, there were eighteen members[12] meeting at the house of Robert Horn, 'old Robin', who had recently settled in the village and had his house licensed as a public meeting place in 1827.[13] Robin and his friends maintained their enthusiasm throughout the 1830s, even though their number declined somewhat, and they were able to build and open a chapel with one hundred and twenty seats in 1839. They also established a Sunday School.[14]

The chapel community pressed on with minor ups and downs until 1858 when numbers rose to around thirty — the result of a fashion for tea. A temperance meeting in March 1858 heard a lecture on total abstinence, Teatotalism had arrived, and sixteen signatures were obtained. Later that year Mr Thomas Lonsdale was given a handsome hymn book in appreciation of his ingenuity in decorating the chapel 'prior to the late tea festival. The Autumn of 1859 saw a tea festival held for the benefit of the Wesleyan Sunday School with an address, singing and recitations by the children.[15]

January 1861 saw a temperance meeting at the schoolroom with Mr C. Walker in the chair. Mr Lonsdale and Mr Kipling, both of Bellerby, gave addresses to a large and respectable audience. W. Favell, H. and W. Spence 'entertained the company by singing melodies'. About this time the Bellerby Singers' Supper took place, when the choir and their friends consumed an 'excellent' meal at the house of Mr Isaac Spence. Anthems were performed to 'a late hour', but all on teatotal principals. That Spring saw Mr Lomax from Manchester, redefine those principals when he lectured at the chapel in April to a 'moderate number' with Henry Spence in the chair. The speaker 'spoke convincingly'.[16]

These were successful years for Methodism at Bellerby. There were some thirty members around 1858 but numbers fell later. We notice '2 backsliders' in 1863 but two classes were prospering under the leadership of brothers Calvert and Spence in 1864. The Wesleyan Missionary Society was always popular in the village and the Calvert family its principal support. The Society sent one shilling most years to Woodhouse Grove Methodist school near Bradford whilst steadfastly ignoring most other outside collections. In 1862 the chapel sent ten shillings to help relieve distress among the cotton operatives in Lancashire.[17]

The Sunday school flourished with some twenty children rising to around fifty in fifteen classes in the late 1870s. These were divided into Bible, Testament and Easy Reading sections with Senior Classes under Mrs Dunkil and Mr T. Lonsdale. In June 1880 the annual Wesleyan Sunday School treat took place at Aysgarth Falls.[18]

Temperance remained fashionable and highly popular for all ages at Bellerby. A tea meeting took place 26 February 1877, presumably at the schoolroom, the venue for the Wesleyan tea party on 22 November that year. The scholars had a one day holdiday for this event in 1878. The annual round included tea in the autumn and a treat in the summer throughout the 1870s and 1880s centred on either the chapel or the schoolroom.[19]

The year 1884 saw something of a fracas regarding 'certain parties' who were at fault over the non payment of seat rents in the chapel. Messrs Cradock and Canon were directed to investigate the matter. Meanwhile Mr Brockell was thanked for his aid in clearing off the chapel debt; the building was insured for £200; and the front of the chapel was rough cast.[20]

Membership fluctuated through these years, settled around fifteen in the 1890s, shot up to twenty plus around 1906, before a gradual decline set in. The families most involved in chapel life around this period were those of Mawer, Brockell, Murray, Spence, Hakin, Russel, Gregg, Walker, Barker, Armistead and Woodward. Storey from Walburn Hall, Simpson, Eyles, Robinson, Ward, Cleminson, Danson and Daykin.[21]

These people met on Whit Sunday, 22 May 1904, for their annual Love Feast, which had replaced the tea festival of former years as the highlight of the year. There was, we are told, a 'goodly number present', the chapel full and the singing lively and inspiring. Tom Summers played the organ. They sang 'good old Methodist tunes' heartily and heard around thirty individuals testify their faith. John Harrison from Horsehouse, preacher for the day, described himself as a 'blundering sort of fellow [but] we thought he rang true'. They remembered the stalwart member Margaret Murray who had died in 1903. So passed Lovefeast Sunday into history.[22]

The chapel continues, as the oldest surviving Methodist Church in the Wensleydale Circuit still in regular use. The fabric was somewhat robbed of its original simplicity by a massive alteration carried through, at a cost of £175, in 1931.[23] The Society maintains its momentum in the village with regular services and a round of events culminating in the harvest festival held in September.

The reconstruction of Bellerby Wesleyan Chapel in October, 1931. This work altered completely the form of the 1839 building. A new entrance with a big porch on the south side replaced the original north door and required the complete reversal of the internal fittings. A communion rail was fitted, so too was a new roof and all the external walls were covered with pebble-dash. Front row left to right: J. T. Leafe, Miss Martha Hird, John Mawer, Mr Hollocks, a Thistlethwaite boy, Alan Singleton. Back row left to right: Fred Walker?, John Scott, Joe Kendray, Jimmy Kendray, Billy Kendray, Tom Graham, George Alderson, Burton Lawson. Tony Gregg Collection.

The summer and autumn of 1844 were marred by an outburst of anti-religious feeling brought on by the appearance of one Joseph Barker in Wensleydale. The first shot came in July when the newly installed curate, Richard Ellis, advertised for a single man to act as parish clerk and schoolmaster at Bellerby, adding 'no followers of the heretic, Joseph Barker of Newcastle need apply'.[24]

The new sect had seceded from the Methodist New Connexion, itself an early break away group from Methodism. There were some Barkerites at Middleham with the possibility of some at Bellerby. The reason for Rev Ellis's exceptionally bitter attitude is never explained. Fletcher Clarke of Hawes, the proprietor of the *Wensleydale Advertiser,* was equally incensed and wrote disparagingly of Barker and 'the detestable doctrines he so unblushingly promulgates in the midst of a christian people'. He was scandalised to find that the Quakers had allowed Barker the use of their meeting house.[25]

The Rev Ellis wrote and Mr Fall of Leyburn printed a broadside consisting of a dialogue in rhyme against Joseph Barker. Furthermore, the curate promised to publish 'a complete exposition of the errors and heresies taught by Barker'.[26] Heady stuff. The new sect, not surprisingly, made a demonstration at Bellerby the last Sunday in September. It was, wrote Fletcher Clarke, 'a failure, and the lecturer was cut up in fine style by some of the audience'.[27] The furor subsided, Richard Ellis left soon after, the Barkerites disappeared and not only from Bellerby.

The initial treatment by 'Bellerbarians' of Quakers, Methodists and Barkerites was remarkably similar through two centuries. It was and is paralleled by the enthusiasm shown for any new venture which found favour with the community, there would be an enthusiastic reception whether good or bad.

9 The School

When the curate, William Kirkbank, drafted his return to Visitation in 1811, he noted 'one voluntary County School, but not endowed, where about 40 Scholars are taught'. Neither teacher nor venue were given then or in the return of 1814 which mentioned two small schools where reading and writing were taught without finance other than 'the quarterly charge', whatever that might have been.[1] Baines Directory in 1823, gave us a name, Leonard Auton, schoolmaster, Bellerby, the first recorded.[2] Things were on the move.

In 1825 there was a 'village school' and a Sunday School with about forty scholars. [3] The first 'School House' was erected in 1832. It was the work principally, of Francis Walker, a local landowner, who provided the site and raised £45. 16. 0. by subscription to build the school. People gave money and/or labour in leading stones and slates or burning lime at the kiln. Timber was brought from Richmond, slates and flags from Gilbert Scar quarry in Coverdale. James Raw built the school for £11. 16. 7. Leonard Raw cut the inscription 'This School Erected A.D. 1832', Peter Dobson glazed the windows and J. Barras made forms for the children and a desk for the teacher. The total cost was £51. 7. 10.[4]

A detailed conveyance and trust deed was drafted. This enabled the Trustees to take charge of the building and the school, to select and appoint (or discharge if necessary) a schoolmaster to teach and instruct thirty poor boys and girls over the age of four years in reading, writing, arithmetic and other useful learning.[5]

School records have not survived from this period but there is in the town a rare and important arithmetic exercise book, the work of Henry Tidyman, a Bellerby boy born about 1828. He would have been well prepared for a career as a general dealer or shopkeeper as all his studies were geared to the purchase or sale of goods in local and distant markets. He mentions tallow, rice and tar, bullocks and Russian skins; Alderney cows at £11. 8. 6. each; gin, Dutch cheese and Lama shawls; Cashmere bracelets cost 2½d each. Chests of oranges; the clothing of charity boys at Mr Dent's shop in Leyburn; firkins of butter, tobacco, beer and cloth are listed. He intended to use Messrs Hutton and Co.'s Bank at Leyburn. A sample account for stockings has a pair in worsted costing 4/6d with others of thread, black silk, mill'd hose, cotton and fine flannel. 'Mr George Tindale Bought of Henry Tidyman', cloth, haberdashery, groceries and a 'bird decoration', whilst corn in Leyburn market sold at 24/2d per quarter.[6]

Also surviving from the school is the sampler worked by Isabella Bell in 1838. It has, beside pattern, letters and figures, the admonition 'Defer not till tomorrow to be wise, tomorrow's sun may never see thee rise.'[7] Isabella Bell stayed in the village as Mrs Spence, but Henry Tidyman left and is lost to us. The long lived Mary Tidyman, grocer and post mistress was almost certainly his grandmother, and, in all probability, his tutor in shop keeping.[8]

There is no full account of the school before 1877 but a few notes have emerged to show that it continued. Joseph Singleton was involved in the building scheme of 1832 and he was given as schoolmaster in 1841, living at the Cross Keys Inn.[9] The position of schoolmaster and parish clerk was advertised in July 1844[10] and this may well have led to the appointment of Thomas Whitfield from Whorlton, who had charge in 1851. Mrs Lydia Allison was also noticed then as School Dame.[11] The village and its school population were struck by typhus in 1856, a disaster compounding those of consumption and diptheria.[12] Thomas Whitfield was still teaching in 1857 in what had become a National School, that is one allied to the Church of England. Miss Jane Plews was then at Bellerby either as assistant or teacher in a dame school.[13] Mr J. Pullan had the school in 1858.[14] The position was advertised again in 1860, for an unmarried man to teach forty scholars for six pounds a year.[15] Jane Plews appears alone as Schoolmistress in 1861.[16]

The enterprise grew and prospered throughout the 1860s and 1870s with building work and extensions undertaken in 1871 and 1891. Mr Francis Walker, the founder and benefactor, died in 1873 leaving the interest from £1200 to the school.[17] The Diocesan inspection and report for November 1873 showed a large decrease in scholars owing to removals.[18] The summer term of 1874 had thirty one pupils on roll, twenty boys paying 1d each week and eleven girls paying 2d. Their ages ranged from four to fourteen years. By 1877 there were thirty-two pupils between four and twelve years each paying one penny per week. This was not collected after Summer 1890. In 1878 the schoolmaster was paid fifty pounds a year, to which the Education Department contributed £30. 13. 2., the first time Government finance entered the school.[19]

This came as a result of a major reorganisation which had been under way from at least November 1876 when the Rev Casey wrote to the Board of Education regarding 'an efficient Elementary school satisfying the conditions of Annual Grants'. By 3 January 1877 he was 'sorry to have to inform you that the schoolmaster...(Mr Seeley?) is still holding on teaching in the school in spite of his notwithstanding our remonstrances with him'. The Trustees had asked for and been refused the key thus 'the Master paralyses all our efforts to get the school forward'.[20]

Bellerby school was built in 1832, had a bell turret from 1871 and a new infant classroom, properly fitted out from 1891. The school began as a private foundation, became a National School and went on to become a voluntary aided Church of England Primary School. It closed in 1985 due to falling rolls and a general reorganisation of primary education provision in lower Wensleydale.

Top. Joseph Price Bowler met with instant success when he began as headmaster at Bellerby School in the Summer term of 1879. This group photograph, taken later that year, shows him, his wife and seventy five pupils in front of the unaltered school building. Kathleen Hodgson Collection.

Bottom. A second print of 1879 shows Mr Bowler with his class of thirty two handsome and well dressed children. One alone, the nine year old William Ridley, front right with a straw hat, has been identified. Kathleen Hodgson Collection.

He was dislodged somehow and Thomas Newton began as master in May and kept a regular log book from 8th June 1877. The schoolroom was cleared out and cleaned, new desks ordered, and certain children placed 'on the charity'. Books were purchased, slates required from home, and the Rev E. Casey, Curate of Bellerby, was brought in to teach Geography, his subject 'England'. The new desks arrived, with smaller ones for the infants in 1891. The walls were whitewashed regularly and the smell in the 'offices' cured with carbolic disinfectant. The lack of washing facilities was decried. Each child contributed 6d per week for coals in winter and six boys gathered ling from the moor for the fires.

Thomas Newton, according to his successor, left the school in a very backward state but very well furnished. Children studied grammar, singing, drawing, scripture, multiplication and geography. They undertook homework with advantage. Sewing was taught by the Mrs Bell, Crees, Robinson and Jones and some parents refused to pay the extra penny for this tuition. Mrs Osborne gave and distributed a sewing prize and infant boys were required to sew and knit. There was much singing of new songs and a gift of the old church harmonium was welcomed till found to be useless. It was repaired.

The H.M.I. reports show marked improvements in the school throughout the 1880s from 'very poor' in 1885 to 'highly satisfactory' in 1889. Slates and paper were both in use in 1890 when the inspector noted the need of desks for the infants, a globe and pleasant pictures. The figure of thirty-two on roll in August 1877 was rising fast, to forty in September and sixty-eight in October. Thereafter it declined in stages to around thirty in 1898.

Attendance was a problem as ever in an agricultural community beset by unfavourable weather for hay making and harvesting, also baking and helping mother. J. Barker was appointed attendance officer and visited every house in the village. Discipline is never mentioned in respect of academic work, but was more concerned with window breaking, stealing apples or 'being rude to a wayfarer'. One boy was 'fetched to school from his own home, where he had gone to hide', by the master and flogged before the school for playing truant. Illness played a major part in absenteeism, notably whooping cough and mumps with closure for measles in 1881. Whooping cough was present almost every year. January and February 1891 were dominated by sickness and influenza and the headmaster noted the death of the young new Vicar, Rev J. H. Bleasdell, who had often visited the school as Correspondent.

Those years saw a regular round of holidays, feasts, festivals and community 'do's'. Four weeks were taken at midsummer, two at

Christmas, one at Easter and one at Whitsuntide covering Bellerby Feast. Odd days were taken for Leyburn Fair, the Church Sunday School or Choir treat, the Wesleyan Tea Party or Annual Treat at Aysgarth Falls and later at Redcar. Swallow's Circus, or Wombwell's Menagerie took half a day as did Ash Wednesday, the Annual Concert, The Cricketers' Supper a wedding party or visits by Harriers or the Wensleydale Beagles. The Agricultural Show at Leyburn was a regular holiday. So too was the Harvest Home Tea, served in the schoolroom, and followed by the Vicar's distribution of buns and tarts etc to the children, during recreation. Mr Benjamin Brockel, school trustee and farmer, came to the school each year from 1886 to 1891 and distributed oranges. A report from 1906 shows the school devoting two hours each week to gardening.

Joseph Price Bowler, who joined the school in 1879, remained as head and continued to 1921. He was followed by three masters in rapid succession, one of whom, we are reliably told, was drummed out of the village, having found disfavour with the community, much as the religious zealots had done in previous centuries. Order returned with the appointment of Mr Raisbeck Bell in 1925.

Bellerby School seniors, with Mr J. P. Bowler, headmaster, c1921.
Front row left to right: John Buck, Bert Madderson, George Fawcett, Tommy Harrison. Second row, left to right: William Thistlethwaite, Doris Ryde, Kathleen Ward, Clara Ward, Violet Beck, Nellie Ward, Clarice Fawcett, Elsie Cranston, Edith Holmes. Third row, left to right: Ron Mawer, Ted Fawcett, Irene Beck, Nora Madderson, Ethel Wilkinson, Olive Fawcett, Tommy Gregg. Back row, left to right: Jimmy Kendray, Charles Madderson, Herbert Thistlethwaite, Tom Holmes, Maurice Cranston. Kathleen Hodgson Collection.

Bellerby School Juniors with Miss Mary L. Mason, c1921.
Front row left to right: Dick Thistlethwaite, Jackie Beck, Jim Milner, Laurie Ward, Frank Thistlethwaite, ? Rowntree. Second row left to right: Anne Thistlethwaite, Rita Thistlethwaite, Lloyd Mawer, Willie Beck, Winnie Rowntree, Mary Rowntree, Ethel Thistlethwaite, Nancy Daykin, Jane Buck, Jack Robinson, Reg Ride. Third row left to right: Lavina Ryde, Stan Fawcett, Hilda Ryde, Michael Ness, Tommy Rowntree, Isaac Buck. Back row left to right: William Loadman, Lillian Coulson, Agatha Ryde, Dorothy Craddock, Freda Cranston, Madge Scott, Kathleen Hodgson. Kathleen Hodgson Collection

The number on roll had grown throughout those years from sixty-three in 1923 to eighty-one in 1933. New desks were supplied in 1922 when classes comprised infants, juniors and seniors. Miss D. M. Wilkinson joined the staff in January 1928 and began a career in the school spanning forty-five years of turmoil and calm. By 1936 falling rolls robbed the school of a class.

Less attention was paid to curriculum in this log but it was clearly broadening its scope. The H.M.I. found arithmetic and history lacking for the more able. From 1921 the older pupils were taken to Leyburn School for woodwork and cookery lessons whilst the infants were 'happily managed and well taught'. Captain Prince, as Physical Training Organiser for the North Riding, visited the school in December 1920. The children took 'drill' in January. Country walks and nature study began about this time. A walk down Mill Lane to look at trees, hedges and flowers culminated in a composition, 'Our Ramble'. Mrs Robinson continued with sewing and an 'Open Day' in 1927 attracted ten mothers into school.

There was no permanent head teacher after 1934 and the unsettled state of the school is reflected in its reports. 'Real effort' was being made but the resulting work was 'moderate' though progress was noted in 'the matter of formal speech'. At least nine individuals occupied the rostrum through these six erratic years. Winter blizzards and summer storms, also the severe influenza epidemic of 1918, took their toll of attendance figures — the Attendance Officer and the Vicar called regularly. Succeeding years saw school closure because of measles, whooping cough, diphtheria and scarlet fever. The School Medical Officer, the Nurse and Dentist appeared in the early 1920s and the children were sent to Leyburn for eye testing.

The annual holidays continued as before — so too did Leyburn Fair and Show and Bellerby Feast. A garden Fete had become a regular event, as had a merit holiday for good attendance. A spate of Royal Weddings ensured odd day holidays and the Jubilee in 1935 took two. The Sunday School trip to Whitley Bay or Scarborough, R.D.C. Elections, the Tournament of Song at Leyburn and the total eclipse of the sun in June 1927 all gave days off. The school closed for an afternoon in 1929 so that staff and scholars might visit the cinema at Leyburn to see the film *Canada Calling*.

September 1st 1939. 'The School was closed this morning according to the Evacuation Scheme'. It reopened two weeks later with thirty-nine evacuated children on roll — eighteen from Gateshead and twenty-one from Sunderland plus their teachers. Local children attended only during the afternoons with fifty or sixty present. A totally new routine was devised to cope with the strain. Local children only were given a half day holiday for Leyburn October Fair. By 6th November the school could report a return to full-time instruction with eighty-six children on roll in three classes mixed local and evacuated thus, 5 - 9 years (33), 10 - 11 years (26), 12 - 14 years (27).

January 1940 was bitterly cold, the number of evacuees had dwindled and an air-raid warning closed the school for an hour on the 29th. The officer in charge of the warning system (a whistle) was the Vicar, by then almost blind. Mr R. S. Lindsley became headmaster 1 April 1940, a position he held until 1952, less five years spent on active service.

Peripatetic, part-time teachers and those from evacuated schools struggled on through the war years. They were stricken by German measles, took in the Jewish refugees, Hans and Rolf, and were disturbed by the 'graveness of the international situation'. There was a nature ramble in May and in July the school closed for a second evacuation — this one dominated by children from Sunderland. Summer Time was extended to November and in January 1941 the children performed a play, *The Butterfly Queen,* at the Memorial Hall.

Gas masks were inspected and waste ground beside the village hall cleared as a school garden. An allotment was rented later. All the children were innoculated against diphtheria. Late summer saw the school declared a 'Second line rest centre for 25 homeless people' — it was never required. All were involved in Wings for Victory in 1943, followed by victory in Europe and Japan. The Memorial Hall opened as a school canteen in July 1945 and the world along with Bellerby returned to a more settled regime.

The post-war calm saw education reorganised under the 1944 Act whereby secondary education became possible for every pupil. Bellerby children first sat the eleven-plus examination in 1948. Those not entering Yorebridge Grammar School stayed on in the village until a new Secondary Modern School was opened at Leyburn in 1959.

Water closets were installed at Bellerby School in August 1962 — they were reported completely frozen up in January 1963. Blizzards affected attendance, especially in 1953 and 1965. Numbers began to fall during the 1950s and led eventually to the closure of the school in July 1985.[21] Public education ceased in the town after one hundred and seventy-five years, one hundred and fifty-three of them in one building.

Masters and Teachers

1823	Leonard Auton
c1832 - c1841	Joseph Singleton
c1851 - c1857	Thomas Whitfield
1858	Mr J. Pullan
1861	Miss Jane Plews
1877	Mr Seeley
1877	Thomas Newton
1878 - 1879	Master (unnamed)
1879 - 1921	Joseph Price Bowler
1921	Mr J. I. Donegan
1921	Eric S. Jackson
1922 - 1925	John W. Sidebottom
1925 - 1934	Raisbeck Bell
1934 - 1939	Peripatetic and Temporary Heads including Ellen P. Blythe, E. Adamson, Rhoda Squires, A. E. Nash, Gladys Strick, Mr Bell, Alexander Duffus, Miss Teasdale, Mrs Jones.
1940 - 1952	Mr R. S. Lindsley (absent 1941 - 46)

1939 - 1946	Evacuated, Peripatetic and Temporary Heads including Miss Edwards, Mr G. E. Greenwell, G. Rawal, Mr F. Bell, V. M. Holyday, Ethel Skilbeck, W. H. R. Davey.
1952 - 1959	Mr H. M. Plant
1959 - 1961	Mrs E. Warriner
1961 - 1965	Mrs N. Thompson
1965	Ruth Walters
1966 - 1978	Miss K. J. Thompson
1978 - 1979	Mrs I. Burdess (Peripatetic)
1979 - 1984	Miss N. Ashworth
1984	Mrs. O. Moses
1984 - 1985	Miss R. Akers

Bellerby School and the great flood of 27 August, 1933. Kathleen Hodgson Collection.

10 Earning a Living

Bellerby was never a rich place even though from time to time wealthy people lived there. Small farms and a high population in a village on the moor edge ensured a rapid turn-over of people and holdings. Farming was always the predominant industry with craft and service occupations intermingled. Rural by-employments were in evidence in all periods.

The records suggest a continual diversification of occupations in the village community through the three centuries covered by the study, c1550 - c1850, but that view may simply reflect more and better evidence from later times. Lesser men hardly ever appear in sixteenth century records whereas they abound in those from the nineteenth. The earlier the date the higher up the social scale are our contacts, the better off only left records but then we have just their view of themselves.

Thomas Metcalfe saw himself as a Gentleman at the Manor House in the 1570s even though he was probably a lawyer. Robert Alcocke the attorney lived at Bellerby in 1600. Adrian Metcalfe, Doctor of Physics, succeeded to the Manor and was sometimes resident there 1647 - 79. The Crosfields of Skelton Cote lived in considerable style towards the end of the century. Francis Crosfield saw himself as a gentleman in 1682 but his family were given to law and diplomacy. George Askew, gentleman of Bellerby, was living in London in 1677. The seemingly large number of Bellerby landlords, often of old village stock, living in the capital gives rise to interesting speculation concerning the reasons for such links and contacts. John Favell, of a well-established old Bellerby family, was resident in London, a yeoman, in 1797. The Crosfields remained as a gentry family at Skelton Cote to around 1731 whilst the Metcalfes, often absent, occupied the Manor House. John Metcalfe was said to be using the chapel privately about 1725 and he appointed a gamekeeper for Bellerby in 1731.[1]

The earliest surviving wills and inventories speak of Bellerby people as yeoman or husbandmen. The Outhwaite family held a leading position among neighbours who occupied what they described as 'fermehold'. This they usually left to their sons in equal portions, (partible inheritance) a practice bound to create small scattered holdings. The term 'husbandman' almost fell out of use after about 1650 but that of yeoman continued and replaced it for all the better off farmers and it persisted to about 1890. Ralph Outhwaite was a husbandman in 1624 whilst Robert Outhwaite, almost certainly his brother, was described as a yeoman.[2] Mathew Webster,

Charles Robinson and Christopher Lonsdale were all active as yeoman in the 1650s.[3] The yeomen family called Fosse left and sold their lands at Brablagill and Blackmoore, Hewbriglees, Crisedelles, Wildflattes, Carkilles, West End, High Pasture and Reddbankes in 1670.[4]

Diversification appears to set in about this time and we find two late references to husbandmen — Ralph Blackburn in 1674 and Christopher Colleson in 1691. This last from his goods — pepper and wire etc, looks more like a shopkeeper or a general dealer.[5] Francis Lonsdale appears as a yeoman in 1682 but his father was by then a whitesmith.[6]

Ralph Ainsley, the Quaker, was blacksmith and whitesmith from mid-century. Henry Skelton was the baker about that time with Matthew Outhwaite a tailor a little earlier and Christopher Dixon a shoemaker somewhat later. John Crosland, father and son are recorded as weavers of woollen cloth in 1747.[7] We know no more of them or their craft until 1772 when Miles Pickersgill, weaver, purchased Johnson's Cottage, beside the road to Leyburn, as a 'cottage house and brewhouse'.[8]

The story of the village inns is far from complete but we must assume that a remote settlement on major routes of communication between two dales and surrounded by market towns would have had inns. Brewers at Bellerby were suppressed and fined in 1655 for selling drink on the Lord's Day and for keeping disorderly houses. The Enclosure Commissioners met throughout 1770 at the house of Elizabeth Marriner which, though not named as an inn, was almost certainly that now known as Kirkbank and sold by Marriner heirs in 1792.[9]

The Court of Quarter Sessions, in 1775, had Joseph Pickersgill, Elizabeth Marriner, Cornelius Durham, Michael Drummond and John Storey 'duly licensed and allowed...to keep a common inn, ale house, or tippling house', at Bellerby — five in all. Elizabeth Marriner disappeared from the Victuallers' Returns in 1777 but Joseph Pickersgill and Cornelius Durham continue until at least 1781. The Manor Court met at Pickersgills' in 1789.[10]

Boar House, the old Favell family property, documented from 1780, is the oldest certain inn in the town. Joseph Miller was there in 1793 and he had, by 1796, a brewhouse which was known as the White Swan Inn by 1805. John Ryder kept it from about 1820, then George Robinson and William Hodgson by 1840. He had changed the sign to Boar Inn by 1851. Henceforth it was known variously as the Boars Head, the Pig and Whistle or just The Pig. It passed via Wetherill, Fawcett and Alderson to its final closure as a public house in 1959.[11]

The site of the Cross Keys Inn was noted as common on the enclosure map of 1773. Henceforth it comprised the allotments of Jones and March and totalled together sixty-four perches. Three tenements, including an inn, were built upon them by one David Yeadon at a date not yet discovered. By 1823 John Thistlethwaite, victualler, was in residence, the sign 'Cross Keys'. Henry Thistlethwaite was there in 1851, Ann Auton in 1861, to be followed by William Stockell — publican and farmer of seventeen acres through several decades.[12]

Bellerby watermill ground corn for at least seven hundred and thirty years before its business stopped in 1926. The machinery was scrapped thirty years later and the stone shell converted into a dwelling in 1972. Much of its early history is linked with the manor and it remained so to at least 1746 when John Metcalfe leased the mill, drying kiln, leat and dams to Thomas Thompson from Coverham. The miller, William Frier, appeared before the manor court in 1797 accused of neglecting the millrace through the town. Ralph Terry took a lease in 1806, his rent, £44 per annum. The Outhwaites as millers had it for several decades and may even have purchased it in 1847. Later millers include Bryan Kay, George and John Raw, and William Scott, the last.[13]

The nineteenth century was the age of the farmer and especially of the improving farmer. A few, such as John Rodwell in 1809, clung to the old yeoman image but William and Thomas Bushby at the Old Hall were content to be described as Farmer in 1833. John Hope Johnson, the new lessee of the Manor farm in 1855, described himself as Gentleman as had Thomas Metcalfe almost three centuries before. Thomas Metcalfe the blacksmith was noted in 1814,[14] then in his prime, the first blacksmith identified since Ralph Ainsley died in 1675. The names of those between are lost.

The year 1814 saw important developments in the high allotments where William Chaytor as Lord of the Manor was busy creating a new deer park. Chaytor was Vice Lieutenant of the North Riding, under the young Duke of Leeds, whose frequent absence from the county left him in charge. It is not unreasonable to assume that his familiarity with Hornby Castle deer park gave both the idea and the stock for the new venture at Bellerby.

The park was created in the lower third of a huge allotment centred on Deepdale, later called Park Gill. It ran to almost 170 acres and included a small plantations of Scots Pine and a hay meadow of about thirty-five acres in the low south-west corner near the Turnpike. Jane and Thomas Douglas and Jane Dolphin made hay there in 1814 but whether yet for deer is not clear.

Raw and Hutchinson built 3137 yards of stone wall with throughs and quoins — throughs cost four pence a load. George Bainbridge carted stone from the old chapel at this time, a limestone quarry was opened and a limekiln built within the park. Surviving portions of the wall show that lime mortar was used in its building as it was in Deer Park House nearby. Men felled trees in the park for gate stoops.

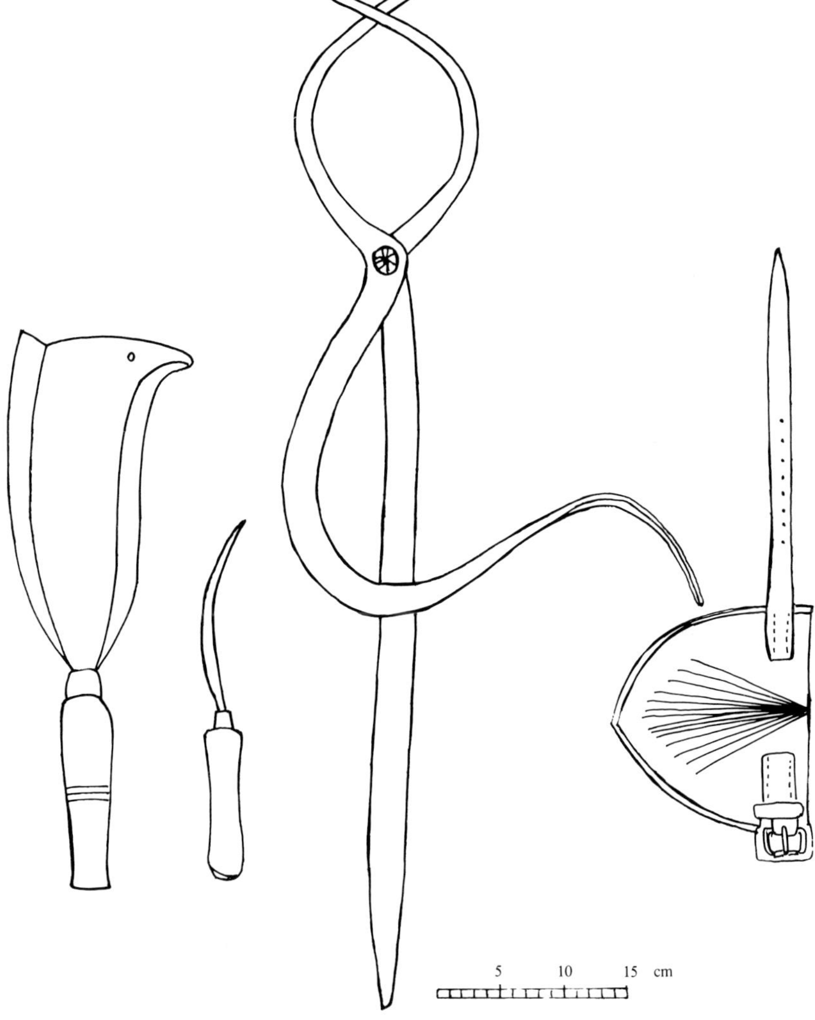

The Gregg family have preserved the besom maker's tools which include a billhook for taking lappings from an ash log and a pricker for fixing them round the head. The besom engine or clamp, formerly spiked into a timber log, was closed by knee pressure on the lever, hence the leather knee pad.

John Hutton of Marske, according to Speight, shot the last wild deer on Bellerby Moor around 1790. The new park deer were introduced about 1814-15 but we have no knowledge of their number or species at that time. John Osborne's lease of the Manor in 1855 reserved to himself all the sporting rights plus the right to keep twenty deer and their produce in Bellerby Park, but at no time was the number to exceed thirty. Edward Hird lived at Deer Park House as Park Keeper in 1851. It was noted 'The Slip Inn' around 1855, was occupied by an agricultural labourer in 1861, and by a gamekeeper in 1871.[15] The demise of the deer is not recorded nor are they remembered.

Georgian times brought much better documentation of the village, its size and social make-up. Charles Raper was the village butcher in 1784. By 1823 there was at Bellerby one gentlewoman, an officiating curate and a schoolmaster with eighteen farmers or yeomen. Several old families including Outhwaite, Lonsdale, Hodgson, Metcalfe and Favell survived. The community was serviced by two blacksmiths and two shoemakers, a corn miller and a cartwright, five stone masons, beside two inn keepers and a common brewer — John Wray at Red Bank.[16]

Besom making came to the town about this time with the arrival from Barden of John Gregg, first documented as a tenant at the Manor Court in 1824. His son, John, also settled at Bellerby as a besom maker and his tools, including the besom engine, billhook, knee pad and pricker all exist today. Heather for besoms was collected from Colsterdale Moor above Masham and ash logs for making lappings for the heads were soaked in Bellerby Beck. There were three besom makers in the village in 1851, four in 1861, but only two in 1871. John Gregg published a note about his besoms in 1858 and this shows them marked J. G., on sale in Richmond market and at Billons in Darlington. The second John was succeeded by his son Thomas, the sole besom maker in 1881, and the last one in the town.[17]

Bellerby's population peaked in 1821 with 402 people in around 100 houses. A minor peak in 1861 had 391 people in 92 houses. Henceforth all was in decline. The nineteenth century censuses present a picture of an almost self-sufficient community stocked with masters and men, labourers, servants, shops and craft workshops. Many of the old buildings which housed those once vital craftsmen are disappearing from the village scene as new houses fill the village centre. The number of services available in this moor edge village in Victorian times is quite remarkable and dual occupations were common.

The seemingly prestigious title of farmer was much sought after up to 1871, often for very small holdings. Six farmers had less than ten acres each that year, seven had between ten and nineteen, three between twenty-one and twenty-seven, six between thirty-eight and sixty-one. Four only had more than 100 acres. By 1881, with agriculture in depression, three survived with less than twenty acres where there had been thirteen ten years previously.

There were two grocer's shops at Bellerby in 1841, three in 1851 and four in 1861. In 1851 Jane Wood and Mary Tidyman doubled as agricultural labourer and post mistress respectively. Thomas Tidyman had charge of the free letter delivery from its inception in 1847. Mary Tidyman was counted as a shopkeeper aged eighty-five in 1871 whilst Margaret Murray had a grocery business at the present-shop. Lonsdale and Hauxwell were butchers, Samuel Saunders a Hawker and General Dealer, whilst Thomas Broadley was a cloth merchant. There had been seven butchers in the town in 1861, including two apprentices. Robert Whitelock and Henry Calvert were butcher farmers. John Wray, common brewer, was noticed in 1841, the last one recorded at Bellerby.

Dress makers were present in numbers — three or four, and sometimes including a seamstress or a neddlewoman, likewise tailors, generally two, including John Watson and Christopher Lye in 1841; Richard Rowntree from Bradford and James Richardson from North Shields in 1881. Shoemakers were numerous until about 1865 after which they virtually disappeared. The straw hat maker, Hannah Metcalfe, was in business in 1841.

There was a concentration of stone masons and builders at Bellerby, usually centred round the families of Jones and Thistlethwaite. The former rebuilt Bellerby and Aysgarth churches; the latter built most of the Victorian and Edwardian houses at Bellerby. Joseph Ryder, father and son, were stone masons in 1851, John Horner, a stone cutter in 1861, may have been responsible for some of the local gravestones though none carry his name. Quarrymen were resident with no less than five in 1871, including Simon Brunskill from Hawes, flag quarry labourer. Ryder's Greygrete millstone quarry on Bellerby Moor is documented from 1844 and the Black Beck sandstone quarries to the west have left extensive spoil heaps near the Grinton road. Dressing sheds and buildings have disappeared from the sites but there was at least one stone mine or 'Level' nearby in the 1850s.

Lead veins were worked to the north and west of Bellerby Parish but nothing bar a few trial shafts had been found within it. Nevertheless lead miners always lived in the town with thirteen present in 1861. This marks an era of prosperity in the lead industry but its impact was confined mainly to two families, the Fowlers from Redmire and the Franklands from Hurst. Each family had a father and three sons aged respectively 19, 17 and 15;

Luke Lonsdale, 1841 - 1906, the Bellerby butcher and pig killer, with four helpers who have not been identified. They use a North Eastern Railway sack barrow as a pig stool n.d. c1900. J. B. Smithson postcard. Tony Gregg Collection

14, 12 and 10. John Bell from Grinton, lead miner, remained in 1881. William Pattison was a coal leader, aged 14, in 1861. Coal mining in the township seems to have ceased by that date as coal miners are not recorded in any census. Progress is noted in the appearance of the plate layers, Metcalfe and Robert Lyall in 1861. The railway had reached Leyburn in May 1856 and with it, no doubt, a ready supply of coal.

The Metcalfes as blacksmiths died out to be replaced by John Scott and Christopher Tidyman by 1841. By 1861 Scott was also farming and the Lyes, George and Christopher, were blacksmithing at Bellerby, as was Richard Graham. William Temple was noted as a wheelright in 1881, to be followed by the joiner-wheelrighting family of Kendray whose workshop stood near Boxwood House. William Rowntree was the 'Pig Jober' in 1881.

That year, 1881, saw two common lodging houses enumerated in the town. One contained, beside the owner's family, a hawker and a labourer with a wife, all from London; a labouring man from Birkenhead; a labourer and his wife from Leeds; and a general labourer from Ireland. The second house had a hawker and his wife from Cumberland; also unmarried men as a labourer from Liverpool, a groom from Leyburn and agricultural labourers from Marrick and Marsett.[18] It was a time of depression in the country at large, especially in agriculture, and this is reflected by people on the move through Bellerby.

Bellerby men working in the stone quarry at Preston under Scar. n.d. c1920. J. B. Smithson postcard. Tony Gregg Collection.

11 Community Life

The spirit of self improvement is never very far from the heart of villages such as Bellerby and it comes as no surprise to find adult education present in the community. Mr J. Pullan, the schoolmaster, started a night school in December 1858 to teach writing and arithmetic each Monday evening from six thirty to nine. He also offered tuition in shorthand.[1] Thomas Newton was similarly occupied in autumn 1877. There was already a public library in the village founded in 1855, with, by 1859, two hundred volumes covering travel, biography, ancient and modern history, religion, astrology, geology, mechanics and the sciences. The year 1858 saw the library committee mount its third tea festival. The Bellerby choristers, led by Mr Wright and assisted by friends from Barden, fourteen altogether, provided the entertainment. There were addresses by the Vicar and other guests and a co-op tea at 4.30 pm, available by ticket, price 9d. The venue was Mr Ryder's long room, formerly the 'ball room for light hearted and nimble footed Bellerbarians [now, in 1859, given up to the] midnight glidings of a pensive ghost — seen only rarely'.[2] The 'long room' is not now recognised or remembered but it may have been the attic room at Old Brooke House, which is claimed by some to have been the Farmer's Arms Inn. The social side of 'Bellerby Library' continued and a note of 1862 shows the committee ordering ingredients for 'Soda Lofe', 'Knode Cake' and 'Lite Cakes' with two pounds of mould candles to light the repast.[3]

Bellerby Feast, held in Whit Week, was in full swing in the 1850s and continues even now. In 1858 the local correspondent of the *Ripon and Richmond Chronicle* complained of the demise of the 'pure character' of the event which had seen Bellerby people making great preparations for visiting friends and relations arriving for 'a time of social enjoyment and rejoicing'. He described how that year young men and boys watched duck and sack races, or dived for coppers in tubs of water etc. There was much drinking, some fighting, and certain parties were despatched to 'quiet apartments' in Leyburn.[4]

The Feast today is a tame affair by comparison. The date has changed to Spring Bank Holiday when a procession of men, behind a big drum is followed round the village by a train of excited girls and boys. They collect money and food in a clothes basket for a meal to be taken in the shade of the Cross Tree on the village green. Sports are held on the playing field later in the day. In the 1920s the adults at the feast wore fancy dress, had their faces coloured blue, and collected the traditional cheesecakes in a clothes basket. The cheesecake tradition has gone, so too have the coloured faces. Rags now pass for fancy dress, but the clowns brush the road with long brooms and hold up holiday traffic through the village.[5]

Bellerby men collecting food, especially cheesecakes, for the Feast. Their progress round the village, led by costumed clowns, was marked by music and noise with much sweeping of doorsteps and paths. Left to right: George Thistlethwaite, William Thistlethwaite, Fawcett, Joe Simpson, Gregg, Tommy Kendray, Joe Kendray, ? , Jack Beck, Harry Thistlethwaite. n.d. c1912. Clarence Thisthlethwaite Collection.

Related to the Feast, in dress and spirit, is the Sword Dance, last performed in 1982/3 but recorded back to 1926/7 and previously, to the 1870s. Photographs of that earlier performance (1872) show the dancers, all men, in costumes and hats decorated with coloured ribbons and cut-out forest animals. The Bellerby sword dance has a King, six Dancers, two Clowns and a Bessie. This last is a man dressed in woman's clothes — the social deviant around which the entire story of good conquering evil revolves amidst dancing with swords and music.[6] Thus was Carnival manifest in the Bellerby community.

Bellerby Reading and Social Club engaged a Quadrille Band for its ball held in the schoolroom in 1905. The club purchased mineral water, bananas, tea and butter, to make a meal and paid a fee for the use of the room. The Vicar was president of the Club. The officers and twenty-nine members were all men. The annual subscription was one shilling and sixpence. There is no trace of a link with the library of former times, for the treasurer bought lamps, four chairs, wallpaper and size, a long settle, three games, a billiard table and paid rent to Mrs Horner. None under fifteen years were to be admitted and the club would close at ten o'clock, ten thirty on Saturday. The *Yorkshire Post* was ordered, and sold to Mr G. Gregg, 'after closing time', also The *Yorkshire Evening Post*. In 1906 a new sign lettered BELLERBY READING AND BILLIARD ROOM was paid for along with metal spittoons and a watering can costing threepence halfpenny.

The club held an annual tea and dance or whist drive for several years and arranged billiard matches with other villages in the area. It was decided to take Mr Deacon's house at a rent of one pound per quarter in 1909. In 1910 a dart board and arrows were supplied and the Club joined the Central Wensleydale Billiard League. The *Yorkshire Post* was stopped in favour of the *Leeds Mercury* and Mr T. W. Grubb, the Rowntree Trust educationalist from Bainbridge, was asked to deliver a lecture in 1912.[7]

That year also saw the rules ratified regarding bad language and rough behaviour, also that none of the village except members were to use the room. Later that year saw a concert and a whist drive was arranged. The next year war broke out and young men were called up so that the club declined so much that 'young ladies' were invited to help with the annual social set for thirtieth of October. They, 'not seeming to care to bother', being involved with various funds re Belgian refugees and a sewing party, the event was cancelled. The club closed down through lack of members — the furniture and effects, books, bookshelves, billiard table and hat rack, were all sold in July 1915.[8] Thus are world events reflected in village life.

The village had seen and celebrated the Coronation of King George Vth, 22 June 1911, with a very splendid 'do'. The school children marched after church from the schoolroom to the Cross Tree for the presentation of commemorative mugs and sports. Tea was prepared for one hundred and fifty adults and sixty scholars, under fourteen years, who sat down at 4 pm to sandwiches, nuts, sweets and oranges. Later the adults enjoyed a knife and fork tea with English beef, roast; home fed ham, boiled; pickles, plain bread, butter and bread, teacakes — plain and currant, buttered, and suitable sweets, 'all to be of the best'. The feast was put out to tender for caterers to provide everything needed to make 'a first class Tea'.[9]

On the other hand the Peace Celebrations of midsummer 1919 were altogether a low key event — the village remembered its losses. A committee met in July, under the chairmanship of Mr J. W. Hodgson, to

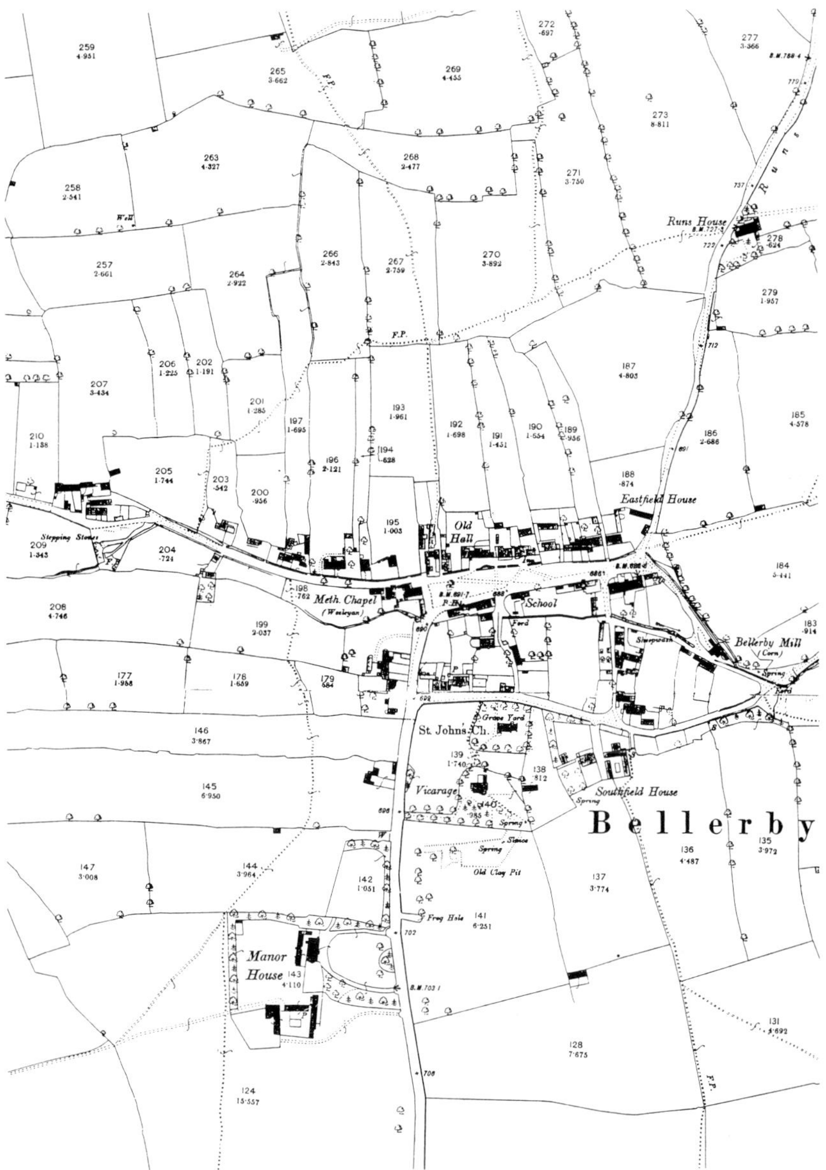

A plan of Bellerby, c1893. Note the stepping stones and footbridge at town head, a ford in the Wynd and a sheepwash near the corn mill. Some twenty ancient house plots, garths or gardens have been built over since this survey was made. Copy from NYCRO.

decide its form. Forty-nine pounds six shillings was raised by collection and subscription and invested in the by now customary knife and fork tea.

The children began proceedings with a procession from school at 2 pm, to the sports, then to tea in the schoolroom at 4 pm. Adults to eat at 5 pm. The ex-servicemen would receive a 'presentation', and the children each a commemorative mug costing ninepence halfpenny.[10]

Prior to 1931 there was no public meeting place in the village. The church, the Wesleyan Chapel and a host of clubs, pubs and private rooms had served that purpose over the years with the school as the principal venue from its erection in 1832.

The present village hall was built as a Memorial Hall or Institute dedicated to the memory of those seven men from the village who died in the Great War. Their photographs are displayed there still. The hall cost £1013.10.6., raised by subscription, fetes and entertainments, the balance of the Peace Celebrations, the Welcome Home Fund and the Reading Room Funds. County Alderman Burrill-Robinson from Redmire performed the opening ceremony and delivered an address. There followed a public tea, a grand concert with R. B. Fawcett and W. H. Breakwell (Humorists) in the evening and a dance at 10 p.m.[11]

From 1931 the Memorial Hall became the centre for community life in Bellerby. A billiard table was purchased at the outset and newspapers ordered — national dailies, evening and *Tit Bits.* A piano was purchased and tuned regularly. The Cricket Club brought its events to the hall, so too did the Mothers' Union. The Annual Concert and Dance took place there in February 1932 and continued thereafter amid whist drives and dances. That year saw electric light installed with power drawn from Mr Hird's private generator. Performances by the Nignogs concert party and the O.K. Band took place regularly plus occasional wedding and funeral feasts. By 1937 we noted the childrens' party, the Womens' Institute, Mothers' Union, a Ladies Keep Fit Class, Cricket Club and the O.K. Band.[12] The Workers' Educational Association held evening classes at the hall from 1938 to 1942. The first of these were a series in local history given by Miss May Bradley from Carperby. Her brief, to judge from the articles she wrote later, was to explore and expand the Victoria County History, local myths and legends, and the vernacular buildings of the town. She clearly recognised the extraordinary richness of Bellerby's buildings, the spirit of independence and the great wealth of documentation.[13] The class moved on later to international affairs.

The advent of war in 1939 brought new outlets as Ambulance classes, Soldiers' Comforts, A.R.P., and the Wesleyan Guild. In May 1942 troops were billeted in the hall with later that year P.O.Ws. The Spring and early

Summer of 1943 were dominated by Wings for Victory. The hall had a new piano, costing £65, Victory Celebrations and the resurrection after the war of some old village institutions alongside some new ones.[14]

Bellerby had had a Cricket Club, on and off, since at least 1848 when a celebratory dinner was recorded. Matches were played against Leyburn, Hunton, Preston and Reeth throughout the 1840s, 50s and 60s, with Bellerby beating Preston by twenty-two runs on 19th July 1860.[15] The club survived but its records, apparently, have not — bar an odd scoring book dated 1939-40, 1946-7. This shows a viable and enthusiastic club in action in 1939, under the captaincy of Mr Raisbeck Bell, and with links across the district to clubs at Redmire, Masham, Spennithorne, Constable Burton, Middleham and Wensley.[16] The cricket pitch at this time was situated in a windy field called Sweats at Cross Head. Later it was moved to a site in the Manor fields beyond the football ground, below the Moor Road. The old tennis courts likewise were situated near the Moor Road, to the north, later moving to Sweats where a splendid timber pavilion was erected.

The cricket club was restarted after the war, unlike those in several local villages, therefore links had to be forged with more distant places such as Arkengarthdale, Newton le Willows, Reeth, Gilling and West Burton. Leyburn, Middleham and Spennithorne resumed as old rivals. Of the nine matches played by Bellerby in 1946 five were won, three lost, and one drawn.[17]

Meanwhile the business of the Memorial Hall continued to expand. Some pre-war institutions were revived, the school canteen moved in in 1945 and a new set of clubs sprang up. These included Girl Guides, Young Farmers and a Football Club. They were joined by a Youth Club and the Bright Hour in 1948, Table Tennis and a Sports Club in 1952. The following year saw Coronation Celebrations, the Mothers' Union, Womens' Institute, the Football Club and Young Farmers continuing along with two more new ventures — Old Time Dancing and Badminton.[18]

A public meeting held 12 October 1951 saw the foundation of a Chess Club, the inspiration of Mr Gifford Brown. It met weekly, on Wednesday, with six boards, in the schoolroom. By 1953 there were seventeen members and a trophy — the Bellerby Cup.[19]

An Amateur Dramatic group flourished as the Bellerby Players around 1959. This group sprang into life following a W.I. Concert Party in 1958. They welcomed all interested players from Bellerby or beyond and mounted their first performance at the Memorial Hall, 28th October 1958. It was a great success and was followed by a fund raising dance and a

Christmas Dinner and Social at the Bolton Arms Hotel. Later shows were taken to Gunnerside and to Quarry Hills, Leyburn. A three-act play was planned for 1959 but this became a one-act play within a concert. By 1960 interest was waning — the socials continued with the promise of 'a show in the Spring', which never materialised.[20]

Thus did village life roll on in change, its course reflecting national events, fashions of popular interest, amusement and entertainment in the country as a whole.

BELLERBY.

You are cordially invited to the

Opening of the New Memorial Hall and Institute

on

Wednesday, January 21st, 1931 at 3 p.m.

by

County Alderman W. R. Burrill-Robinson Esq. J.P.,

of Redmire.

To be followed by a Musical Programme.

A PUBLIC TEA AT 4 P.M.

Tickets 1/- each. Children 6d.

A GRAND CONCERT AT 7-30 P.M.

ARTISTES :

Miss Renee Raymond, Mezzo-Soprano of the London and Provincial Concerts, in songs grave and gay.

Mrs. H. Wood and Miss Wilkinson, Sopranos.

Mr. Ron A. Roberts, Solo Violinist, Rotherham,
(Pupil of Sara Fennings.)

Mr. Wallace Kilding, Baritone.

Messrs. R. B. Fawcett and J. H. Breakwell, (Humorists.)

At the Piano – Miss Minna Wood, Rotherham.

Doors open 7 p.m.

Reserved seats 1/6. Second seats 1/2. Children 6d.

DANCE AT 10 P.M.

Refreshments at reasonable charges. Tickets 1/6 each.

Prizes for Dancing Competition.

Music by LEEMING BAR DANCE BAND.

PLEWS & SONS, Electric Printers, LEYBURN.

The Memorial Hall opening programme, 1931. Kathleen Hodgson Collection.

References and Notes

Abbreviations

Baines. Edward Baines: *History, Directory and Gazetter of the County of York,* 1823.
B.I. Borthwick Institute of Historical Research, St Anthony's Hall, York.
Bulmer. Thomas Bulmer: *History, Topography and Directory of North Yorkshire,* 1890.
CCRO. Cheshire County Record Office, The Castle, Chester.
CRO. County Record Office.
DST. *Darlington and Stockton Times.*
EYC. *Early Yorkshire Charters.*
LCLA. Leeds City Library Archives, Sheepscar Branch Library, Chapeltown Road, Leeds, LS7 3AP.
NR. North Riding.
NRRD. North Riding Registry of Deeds (NYCRO)
NRRS. *North Riding Record Series.*
NS. New Series.
NYCRO. North Yorkshire County Record Office, County Hall, Northallerton, DL7 8AD.
OS. Ordnance Survey.
PRO. Public Record Office, Chancery Lane, London, WC2A 1LR.
RC. *Rievaulx Chartulary.*
RRC. *Ripon and Richmond Chronicle.*
RS. *Record Series.*
SS. Surtees Society.
VCH. *Victoria County History.*
WA. *Wensleydale Advertiser.*
YAS. Yorkshire Archaeological Society, Claremont, Clarendon Road, Leeds, LS2 9NZ.
YASJ. *Yorkshire Archaeological Society Journal.*

Chapter 1. The Setting Pages 1 - 5.

1 O.S., Geological Survey, Sheet 41, *Richmond,* (Solid), 1970.
2 Fieldwork and finds: Mr A. Pratt, Studdah Farm, Bellerby.

3 Axe and report: Mr D. Thistlethwaite, South Dyke Farm, Bellerby.
4 Yorkshire Museum, BCC 707, found and presented by Mr Robinson Craddock, 1875.
5 Found by Mr F. Pearson, Bellerby: *Darlington and Stockton Times,* 9 February, 1957, 6; *The Wensleydale Society Report,* 1960 - 61, 9.
6 William Horne: 'Prehistoric Remains Recently Discovered in Wensleydale', *Proceedings Yorkshire Geological Society,* N.S., IX, 1885 - 87, 175 - 79.
7 O.S., 25 inch map, *Yorkshire, North Riding,* 73/11 (1929); O.S. Archaeological Section pers. comm., 1983.
8 Dr Arthur Raistrick, pers. comm., 1983.
9 Retained by Mr B. Jefford, Leyburn.
10 Sidney Jackson: *Celtic and other stone heads.* Shipley, 1979.
11 *RRC,* 14 March 1874, 5. Bulmer, p370; A. H. Smith: *The Place Names of the North Riding of Yorkshire,* 1928, 252; c.f. River Belah, Brough, Cumbria, in Kenneth Cameron: *English Place-Names,* 1961 (1977), 161.
12 *VCH, Yorkshire,* 2, 237.
13 NYCRO, ZDX 14.
14 *Y.A.S., R.S.,* 21, 1896, 103; *Y.A.S., R.S.,* 74, 1929, 127; Robin E. Glasscock: The Lay Subsidy of 1334, 1975, 373; R. Fieldhouse and B. Jennings: *A History of Richmond and Swaledale,* 1978, 51 - 62.

Chapter 2. Bellerby Takes Shape Pages 6 - 10.

1 *VCH, NR,* I, 260.
2 NYCRO, ZDX 1 - 46; *VCH, NR,* I, 260.
3 *VCH, NR,* I, 260.
4 The Skelton Cote boundary as set out about 1190 - 92, including common and common rights, might be interpreted thus. From Huntergathe (Barden Lane east of Terry's building) by the old embankment to Wyselapeltre (south of Skelton Cote at Hewbriggs Lane gate). North west by the dyke (stone wall) to the green road to Waleburn (Runs Lane Head and the bridle road) to the Caldekelde (Mary Morland's Well). Forward to and down Uluedalebec (Spring Gill) to join the green road to Bostscalebec (foot path to Boston Farm) then down Bostscalebec (Boston Beck) to Huntergathe (Walburn Lane near Boston Bridge) then south to Barden Lane.
5 NYCRO, ZDX 29; *EYC,* 5, 103 - 4; *VCH, NR,* I, 258, 260.

6 *RC, SS,* 83, 1889, 399; William Burton, Monasticon Eboracense, York, 1758, 359.
7 *RC,* 103-5; *EYC,* 4, 123; *VCH, NR,* I, 261.
8 NYCRO, ZDX 138; L. P. Wenham, NYCRO *Journal,* 8, 1981, 35 - 36, 50 - 53.
9 *VCH, Yorkshire,* 3, 1913, 160 - 61; *EYC,* 4, 33.
10 NYCRO, ZDX 7; *VCH, NR,* I, 260.
11 NYCRO, ZDX 8.
12 *EYC,* 4, 104; Ibid 5, 83 - 4; *VCH, NR,* I, 261.
13 NYCRO, ZDX 29; *EYC,* 5, 103 - 4; *VCH, NR,* I, 258. Burton, ibid; *RC,* ibid.
14 *YAS, RS,* 81, 1931, 9.
15 NYCRO, ZDX 68, 75, 78, 105, 108.
16 NYCRO, ZDX, charters and deeds.
17 NYCRO, ZDX 20.
18 NYCRO, ZDX 12.
19 NYCRO, ZDX 33.
20 NYCRO, ZAZ.
21 NYCRO, ZAZ.
22 *YAS, RS,* 17, (1894), 1895, 48.
23 NYCRO, ZDX Manor Court Roll, 16 May 1443.
24 NYCRO, ZDX 71.

Chapter 3. 'Howseling People' Pages 11 - 19.

1 NYCRO, ZDX 108.
2 NYCRO, PR/SPE Spennithorne Parish Registers. *NRRS,* 5, 1889, 210. *Leeds Parish Register,* I, 62.
3 Bellerby Parish Chest. Burial Registers.
4 LCLA, RD/AP 1 Wills and inventories, 1535 - 1697.
5 J. A. Twemlow: *Papal Letters 1471 - 85,* 1955, 383 - 4.
6 S.S., 91. 1894, 116.
7 PRO, E. 179/216/462.
8 CCRO, EDV 7, 1789 - 1825.
9 PRO, Census. 1841, HG 107/1254; 1851, HO 107/2379; 1861, RG 9/3669; 1871, RG 10/4869; 1881, RG 11/4874.

Chapter 4. Fields and Farming Pages 20 - 27.

1 NYCRO, ZDX 71.
2 ” ” 72 - 3.
3 LCLA, RD/AP 1. Thomas Metcalfe 1575, Anthony Outhwaite 1579, Ralph Outhwaite 1624, Robert Outhwaite 1625.
4 LCLA, RD/AP 1. Ralph Blackburn 1674, Jerome Robinson 1684, Francis Morland 1686, Christopher Colleson 1691, Edward Favell 1694, Christopher Dixon 1697.
5 NYCRO, *Journal* 8, 1981, 53.
6 ” ZDX 139.
7 ” Z 100.
8 Deeds, Mr W. E. Pratt, Fryer Ings, Bellerby.
9 NYCRO, ZDX 130 - 1, 133 - 5, 137 - 9.
10 ” ” 133 - 4.
11 ” ” 132 - 3.
12 ” ZPT IV/2/5/1/1; I/BEL(PC/BEL); NRRD BB 20/28 - 64.
13 O.S. *Yorkshire (N.R.)* 6″ map, 1857, (Surveyed 1854); NYCRO, ZDX 122.
14 Deeds, Mrs M. Clarke, Fern Cottage, Bellerby.
15 ” Mr A. Pratt, Studdah Farm, Bellerby.
16 NYCRO, ZDX 125 - 6.
17 Deeds, Mrs M. Clarke; *RRC,* 6 Nov. 1858.
18 *RRC,* 30 Jan. 1858.
19 *RRC,* 14 May 1859, 21 Jan. 1867.
20 *RRC,* 8 Sept. 1860, 1 Sept. 1860, 6 Oct. 1860, 9 Feb. 1867, 20 Oct. 1860; *DST* 10 Sept. 1870, 24 Sept. 1870.

Chapter 5. Some Lords — Pages 28 - 33.

1 *VCH, NR,* I, 324.
2 Marie Hartley and Joan Ingilby: *Yorkshire Portraits,* 1961, 3 - 8.
3 *VCH, NR,* I, 260, 324.
4 NYCRO, ZDX Manor Court Rolls and Papers.
5 ” ibid.
6 Essex CRO., Barrett-Lennard MSS, D/DL 1947.
7 ” ” ” ” ” 1511. LCLA, RD/AP 1, Elizabeth Symson, 1535.
8 Joseph Foster: *Glover's Visitation of Yorkshire,* 1584-5, 1875, 249.
9 LCLA, RD/AP 1, Thomas Metcalfe, 1575; S.S., 26, 1853, 256 - 58.

10 *VCH, NR,* 2, 260; NYCRO, ZDX, 59 - 62, 64 - 5, 67.
11 NYCRO, ZDX 48 - 9, 51, 55 - 6, 69.
12 York Minster Library, Hailstone, Box 5.34; NYCRO, ZDX 71.
13 NYCRO, ZDX, 75.
14 ” ” 132 - 33, ZAW.
15 ” ZPT IV/2/5/1 - 9.

Chapter 6. And Men. Pages 34 - 39.

1 NYCRO, PR/SPE 1/5; *Charity Commissioners' Reports,* Yorkshire North Riding, 1819 - 1837, 704 - 5.
2 *RRC,* 5 Dec. 1874; Charity Minute and Account Books, Mrs E. Scott, Bellerby Manor.
3 York Minster Library, Hailstone 4/33.
4 NYCRO, ZDX Manorial, 1760, 1764.
5 ” ” ” 1764.
6 *NRRS,* 8, 1890, 173, 238, 246.
7 NYCRO, ZDX Manorial, 1766.
8 ” ZQH 11/2/24.
9 ” ZDX Manorial n.d.
10 ” ” ” 1789, ZIF 657.
11 ” ” ” 1809.
12 ” ” ” 1819 - 1824.
13 ” ” ” 1863.
14 ” ” ” Boundary Roll 1863; NRRD, JB 549 822; J. B. Radcliffe: *Ashgill or the life and travels of John Osborne,* London, 1900.
15 *RRC,* 9 Feb. 1867.
16 NRRD, 1218, 212, 100.
17 Information supplied by Mrs Mary Clarke, Fern Cottage, Bellerby.

Chapter 7. St John's Church. Pages 40 - 48.

1 Bulmer, 370, 596.
2 NYCRO, ZDX 7, 19, 22, 37; *VCH, NR,* I, 260, 264; Harry Speight: *Romantic Richmondshire,* 1897, 372 - 4; *SS,* 94, 1897, 11.
3 NYCRO, ZDX Bellerby Court Rolls 1418 - 71; V. H. H. Green: *Spennithorne Church Guide,* nd, 5; J. A. Twemlow: *Papal Letters 1471 - 85,* 1955, 383 - 4; BI, Archbishop's Register 1465 - 76.

4 SS, 91, 1984, 116; *VCH, NR*. I, *YASJ*, 20, 1908, 360; NYCRO, ZDX, 71, 194.

5 NYCRO, PR/SPE 1573 — date; BI, R III W, Catterick 26.

6 CCRO, EDA 3/3, 334; NYCRO, I/BEL (PC/BEL); Ripon Diocesan Registry, Bellerby Deeds, 1874; *RRC*, 14 March 1874, 5.

7 CCRO, EDA 1/7, 153, 1/9, 124, 126, 183, 1/10, 2, 6, EDV 7, 1789, 1804, 1811, 1814, 1821, 1825; LCLA, CD/PB 2 Bellerby; L. P. Wenham: 'Letters of James Tate', *YAS, RS*, 128, (1965). 1966, xi, 6 - 8, 19.

8 CCRO, EDA 1/9, 37, 133, 161 - 2, 1/10, 19, EDV 1821, 1789, LCLA.CD/PB Bellerby; Cumbria CRO, pers. comm. 1984.

9 CCRO, EDV 7, 1825; NRRD, CG. 949. 654; LCLA, RD/AP 1. William Kirkbank 1843; NYCRO, PR/SPE; Mary Thistlethwaite: 'Kirkbank House', *Bellerby 1*, 1983; *WA*, I, 16 July 1844, 58; Bellerby Parish Chest, Burial Register 1847 - date.

10 *RRC*, 14 March 1874, 5; NYCRO, ZQH 11/2/24; PR/SPE 1/4; Ripon Diocesan Registry, Bellerby Deeds, 1847; *The London Gazette*, 2 May 1848; Harry Speight: *Romantic Richmondshire*, 1897, 372 - 74.

11 NYCRO, PR/SPE 1/10; LCLA, CD/PB 2 Bellerby; CCRO, EDA 1/11, 387, 394, 1/12, 9; Alfred Gatty: *A life at one living*, 1884, 20; *Dictionary of National Biography*, Supplement 1901 - 11, 1920, (1927), 1; Sheffield City Library, HAS 40 - 84; Christabel Maxwell: *Mrs Gatty and Mrs Ewing*, 1949; *WA*, I, 26 March 1844, 16 July 1844; PRO, Census 1851; *DST*, 19 July 1890.

12 LCLA, CD/PB 2 Bellerby; CCRO, EDA 1/10, 193 - 4, 1/11, 160; Bellerby Parish Chest, Baptism and Burial Registers 1847 - date; Pers. comms. Mr T. Cockerill to Mary Thistlethwaite, 1977 & Mr L. J. Latham to D.S.H., 1982; PRO, Census 1851 and 1861; *RRC*, 28 March 1874.

13 *RRC*, 13 April 1861.

14 *RRC*, 14 March 1874, 28 March 1874; Bulmer, 370; Ripon Diocesan Registry, Bellerby Deeds 1874.

15 Bellerby Parish Chest, Service Register 1880 - 1928; Pers. comms. T. Cockerill and L. J. Latham, ibid; Mary Clarke: 'Happy Days and Endless Work,' Mary Thistlethwaite: 'Saga of a Country Churchyard,' *Bellerby 2*, 1984.

Chapter 8. Catholics and Nonconformists. Pages 49 - 55.

1 Hugh Aveling: *Northern Catholics — The Catholic Recusants of the North Riding of Yorkshire,* 1558 - 1790, 1966, 175, 239, 263, 359, 390; Winifred I. Haward: *The Secret Rooms of Yorkshire,* 1956, 47 - 50, Clapham; Bulmer, 482 - 84.
2 Aveling: 390.
3 CCRO, EDV 7, 1789, 1804, 1811, 1821, 1825.
4 *NRRS,* 7, 1889, 70, 102.
5 Richard Robinson: *A Blast blown out of the North,* 1680, 5 - 9.
6 ibid 31 - 2.
7 NYCRO, R/Q/R 16/9.
8 CCRO, EDV 7, 1789, 1804, 1811, 1814.
9 Edmund Peacock: *Recollections of the Rise and Progress of Methodism in Wensleydale,* 1872, Darlington, 7 - 10.
10 CCRO, EDV 7, 1789, 1804, 1811, 1825.
11 Harry Holroyd (Ed): *Methodism in Wensleydale,* 1765 - 1965, Leyburn, 1965, 7.
12 Peacock, p 34; NYCRO, R/MC/W 1/1.
13 ” p 34, 77; LCLA, RD/RM 1/64.
14 ” p 34.
15 *RRC,* 27 March 1858, 20 Nov. 1858, 12 Oct. 1859.
16 *RRC,* 26 Jan. 1861, 13 April 1861.
17 NYCRO, R/MC/W 1/18.
18 Bellerby Sunday School Teachers' Meeting Minute Book, 1877 - 78, Mr A. & Mr J. Pratt, Studdah Farm, Bellerby.
19 Bellerby C.E. School Log Book, 1877 - 94, Mrs M. Clarke.
20 Bellerby Methodist Chapel Trustees Meeting Minute Book, 1884 - 94, A. & J. Pratt.
21 NYCRO, R/MC/W 1/21; Bellerby Class Book, 1892 - 1911, A. & J. Pratt.
22 *The Wensleydale Wesleyan Methodist Monthly,* 4, July 1904.
23 Bellerby Chapel accounts for alterations, 1931, A. & J. Pratt.
24 *WA,* 16 July 1844.
25 ibid, 10 Sept. 1844.
26 ibid, 8 Oct. 1844.
27 ibid, 8 Oct. 1844.

Chapter 9. The School. Pages 56 - 65.

1 CCRO, EDV 7, 1811, 1814, 1821.
2 Baines, 414.
3 CCRO, EDV 7, 1825.
4 Bellerby Parish Chest. School Subscription and Building Accounts, 1832 - 33. Copy with Miss K. I. Hodgson, Aston House, Bellerby.
5 Bellerby Parish Chest. School Trust Deed, 1832, Charity Commissioner's Copy from the Close Roll, 1876.
6 Henry Tidyman's School Exercise Book, 1838 - 39. Miss K. I. Hodgson.
7 Isabella Bell's Sampler, 1838. Miss K. I. Hodgson. Bellerby.
8 PRO, Census 1841 - 71.
9 " " 1841.
10 *WA,* 16 July 1844.
11 PRO, Census 1851.
12 Bellerby Parish Chest. Burial Register, 1847 - date.
13 Kelly, *Post Office Directory, N & E.R. Yorkshire,* 1857, 1498.
14 *RRC,* 11 Dec. 1858.
15 Ibid, 12 May 1860.
16 PRO, Census 1861.
17 RRC, 5 Dec. 1874.
18 Ibid, 1 Nov. 1873.
19 Bellerby School Pence Account Book, 1874 - 77; School Treasurer's Cash Book, 1877 - 96. Miss K. I. Hodgson.
20 PRO, ED 21/19351.
21 Bellerby Church of England Primary School Log Books, 1877 - 94; (1894 - 1918 not present) 1918 - 69; 1969 - 85. Made available by Mrs O. Moses.

Chapter 10. Earning a Living. Pages 66 - 73.

1 LCLA, RD/AP 1, Thomas Metcalfe, 1575; SS, 26, 1853, 256 - 58; NYCRO, ZDX 69, 97, 107-08; LCLA, RD/AP 1, George Askew, 1677; Studdah Deeds; NYCRO, ZDX 130 - 31. 135 - 39; York Minster Library, Hailstone 4/33; NYCRO, ZAF 4.
2 LCLA, RD/AP 1, Elizabeth Symson, 1535, Randolph Stele, 1577, Anthony Outhwayte, 1579.

3 LCLA, RD/AP 1, Robert and Ralph Owthwaite, 1624 - 25; NYCRO, ZDX 100, 105 - 06.
4 NYCRO, Z 178.
5 LCLA, RD/AP 1, Ralph Blackburn, 1674. Christopher Colleson, 1691.
6 NYCRO, ZDX 108.
7 NYCRO, R/Q/R 16/9, ZB 34, ZDX 29, ZB 104.
8 Conveyance 14 April 1722, Mrs. M. Thistlethwaite, Prospect House, Bellerby.
9 *NRRS,* 5, 1887, 251, 255; NYCRO, ZPT IV 2/5/1-9; NRRD, CG 494 654.
10 NYCRO, QDL (V) 1/2/8; ZIF 657.
11 Deeds, Mr and Mrs W. Alderson, Boar House, Bellerby; Baines, 414; PRO, Census 1841 - 71; Bulmer, 370.
12 NYCRO, I/BEL (PC/BEL); Abstract of Title, Mrs. A. Hartley, Cross Keys, Bellerby; Baines 414; PRO, Census 1841 - 81; Bulmer, 370.
13 *VCH, NR,* I, 258; Information from Mr W. Scott, Far Ende, Bellerby; NYCRO, ZB 103, ZDX Manor Court Roll 1797, ZIF 659; *WA,* 15 Jan, 1847; Rate Book, 1872, Miss K. I. Hodgson, Aston House, Bellerby; Bulmer, 370.
14 Conveyance, 12 May 1809, Miss K. I. Hodgson. NYCRO, ZIF 663; Deeds, Mrs M. Clarke, Fern Cottage, Bellerby; NYCRO, ZDK 180.
15 Information regarding William Chaytor and the Vice Lietenancy from M. Y. Ashcroft, County Archivist; NYCRO. ZDX 175, 183 - 91, 194 - 95, 200 - 01; Harry Speight, *Romantic Richmondshire,* 1897, 372 - 74; Deeds, Mrs M. Clarke. PRO, Census 1851 - 71.
1851 - 71.
16 NYCRO, ZIF 656; Baines, 414.
17 Information from Mr T. G. Gregg, South View, Bellerby; NYCRO, ZDX Manor Court Roll 1824; PRO, Census 1851 - 81; *RRC,* 30 Oct. 1858.
18 PRO, Census 1801 - 81; *WA,* 7 Dec. 1847, 8 Oct. 1844; Ordnance Survey six inch map, *Yorkshire (N.R.) Sheet 53,* 1857 (Sur, 1854); C. S. Hallas: *The Wensleydale Railway,* Clapham, 1984, 10.

Chapter 11. Community Life. Pages 74 - 80.

1 RRC, 11, 18 Dec. 1858.
2 Ibid, 1 Jan. 1859.

Haull, Thomas, 15.
Hauxwell, 3.
Hauxwell family, 71.
Hawes, 20, 50, 71.
Heather, ling and turf, 2, 20, 22, :2, 32-3, 39, 60, 70.
Helbeck, Thomas, 6.
Heslop, William, 46.
High Beck, 36, 38.
Hird: Edward, 70; Mr, 78.
Hodgson: family, 70; Andrew, 17; James, 27; James W, 76; Thomas, 15; William, 28, 38, 67.
Howseling people, 18, 41.
Hogarth, John, 42, 45.
Holmes, Richard, 25.
Hop, Margaret, 32.
Horn, Robert, 52.
Hornby Castle, 68.
Horner: John, 71; Mrs, 76
Horsehouse, 53.
Horticulture, 27, 30, 33, 37, 64, 68.
Houses and farms: Aston House, 14; Beckside, 14; Bellerby Moor, 25; Bellvue Terrace, 14; Black Beck, 19, 23; Boar House, 14, 67; Boxwood, 72; Brookside, 14; Church View, 12, 14; Corner Cottage, 11-13, 19; The Cornmill, 28-30, 68; Deacon House, 14; Deer Park, 68-70; Eastfield, 14; East Grange, 14; Fern Cottage, 9, 12, 14, 16; Fryer Ings, 7-8, 21; Gatelands, 18; Hall Garth, 10, 12, 14; The Old Hall, 2, 11-13, 18, 68; Halfpenny House, 3, 7, 31; High Farm under Whitfield, 25-6; Hilltop, 14; Hobthrush, 23; Johnsons Cottage, 67; Kirkbank House, 14, 45, 67; The Lilacs, 14; Lonsdale House, 14; The Manor House, 2, 11, 15, 18, 20-1, 23, 26-7, 30, 37-8, 49, 66, 68, 70, 79; The Nook, 12; Old Brooke House, 14, 74; Old Post Office, 14; Pear Tree Cottage, 14; Prospect Farm, 14; Prospect House, 14, 23; Red Bank, 9, 23, 70; Rose Cottage, 14; Rowantrees, 14; Rustic Cottage,
Houses & Fields *(continued)* 14; Scotts Cottage, 12; The Shop, 14; Skelton Cote, 5-8, 10, 15, 18, 21-2, 31, 34, 38, 41, 66, 82; Slip Inn, 70; South Dyke, 2, 19, 23; Southfield, 9, 14, 38; South View, 11; Spring Cottage, 14; Studdah, 12, 16, 18; The Terrace, 14; Town Head, 14; Turnpike Bar, 19; Vicarage, 14, 40, 46; Vine House, 14; Walburn Hall, 6, 31, 53; Westfield, 14; White House, 23.

Howardian Hills, 2.
Hudson, James, 32.
Hunton, 79.
Hurst, 71.
Hutchinson and Raw, 68.
Hutchinson, Matthew, 50.
Hutton and Co, 56.
Hutton, John, 70.

Ianson: James, 50; Margaret, 15; William, 22.
Inns: Boar, 67; Boars Head, 67; Cross Keys, 14, 57, 67-8; Drummonds, 67; Durhams, 67; Farmers Arms, 74; The Long Room, 74; Marriners, 67; Pickersgills, 37; The Pig, 67; Pig and Whistle, 67; Slip Inn, 70; Storeys, 67; White Swan, 67.
Ireland, 72.

Jackson, Sidney, 4.
Johnson: John, 15; John Hope, 68.
Jones: family, 67, 71; George, 32; J., 47; Mrs, 60.

Kay, Bryan, 68.
Kendray (Kendrew): family, 72; Anne, 15; James, 17; Luce, 15; William, 15.
Kipling, Mr, 52.
Kirkbank: Elizabeth, 45; Nancy, 45-6; William, 45-6, 49, 52, 56.
Knaresdale, 45.
Knights Templars, 40.

Lake District, 2, 5.
Lancashire, 52.
Lascelles, 20.
Lead mining, 71-2.
Lee, jockey, 27.
Lee, coal miner, 32.
Leeds, 15, 50, 72.
Leeds, Duke of, 68.
Leeds Mercury, 76.
Leyburn, 2-4, 10, 27, 46-7, 49-50, 54, 56, 61-4, 67, 72, 74, 79, 80.
Library and Reading Room, 74-6, 78
Limestone and limekilns, 2, 23-5, 56, 68-9.
Lincolnshire, 27, 30.
Lindsley, R. S., 63.
Linsley: Anne, 15; Betty, 15; William, 15.
Liverpool, 72.
London, 30, 66, 72.
London Gazette, The, 46.
Longlands, John, Silversmith of Newcastle, 45.
Longstaffe family, 15.
Lonsdale (Lonsdell): family, 70-1; Edmond, 15, 38; Edmund, 28; Charles, 41; Christopher, 67; Francis, 36, 67; Luke, 72; Matthew, 12, 18; Thomas, 52-3.
Lorimer, John, 40.
Lyall, Robert, 72.
Lye, Christopher, 71-2; George, 72.

Manchester, 52.
Manners, Nicholas, 50.
Manor (Bellerby): 4, 6, 20, 28, 30-2, 34, 36-8, 40-1, 66; Court, 28-9, 35-8, 40-2, 67-8, 70.
March: family, 67; James, 36;
Phyllis, 14; Richard, 14, 36.
Marrick, 50, 73.
Marriner: Elizabeth, 67.
Marsett, 73.
Marske, 70.
Mary Morlands Grave, 8, 10, 31-2, 82
Masham, 7, 15, 28, 50-1, 70, 79.
Mawer family, 53.
Maynerd, John, 15.
Memorial Hall, 63-4, 78-80.
Metcalfe: family, 30-1, 45, 49, 66, 70, 72; Adrian, 31, 66; Christopher, 32; Francis, 20, 30, 41; Hannah, 71; John, 31, 33-6, 42, 66, 68; Kathleen Jackson, 30; Luke, 30; Matthew, 30; Mr, 23; Nicholas, 30; Thomas, 17, 20, 30-1, 66-68.
Methodism, 34, 49, 52-5, 78.
Middleham, 3, 34, 40, 54, 79.
Middleton Tyas, 46.
Mill Beck (Millrace), 2, 37, 68.
Miller, Joseph, 67.
Millom, 45.
Millstones, 71.
Milner: James G., 17, 27, 45; Nancy, 45-6; William K., 45.
Morland: Ann, 14; Francis, 14, 17, 21, 32; Mary, 31-2; Richard, 20.
Mowbray, Vale of, 2.
Murray: family, 53; Margaret, 53, 71.
Musard, Enisan, 4, 6-7.
Music, song and dance, 46, 52, 60, 74-5, 78, 80.

Nappa Hall, 30.
Newcastle, 42, 45, 59.
Newton-le-willows, 79.
Newton, Thomas, 60, 74.
Neville family, 34.
Nichols, Francis, 22.
Night School, 74.
Nonconformity, 42, 48-55.
Northallerton, 27, 30.
North Riding, 15, 49, 51, 62, 67-8.
North Shields, 71.
North Yorkshire, 2.

Occupations: Agricultural labourer, 70-1, 73; Attorney, 66; Bailiff, 28, 36, 38; Baker, 67; Besom maker, 17, 36, 69-70; Blacksmith, 50, 67-8, 70, 72; Brewer, 67, 70-1; Brickmaker, 14; Builder and stone mason, 11, 15, 70-1; Butcher, 70-1; Bylawman, 28, 36; Cartwright, 70; Cloth merchant, 71; Coal leader,

Occupational *(continued)*
72; Corn miller, 70; Constable, 6; Doctor, 66; Dressmaker, 71; Farmer, 19, 68, 70-2; Flag Quarry labourer, 71; Gamekeeper, 28, 36, 66, 70; Gentleman/woman, 66, 68, 70; General dealer, 71; Groom, 72; Hawker, 71-2; Herdsman, 23; Husbandsman, 30, 66-7; Inn keeper, 70; Jockey, 27; Joiner, 72; Labourer, 72; Lapidary, 19; Lawyer, 28, 30, 66; Lead miner, 71; Maltster, 22; Needlewoman, 71; Officiating Curate, 70; Overseer, 34, 37; Parish Clerk, 54, 57; Park keeper, 70; Pig jobber, 72; Pinder, 28, 38; Plate layer, 72; Post mistress, 57, 70; Quarryman. 15, 71, 73; School teacher, 54, 56-7. 74; Seamstress, 71; Shoemaker, 18, 67, 70-1; Shopkeeper, 56, 71; Soap boiler, 36; Staffheard, 23; Steward, 28, 31, 36-8; Surveyor, 38; Straw hat maker, 71; Tailor, 67, 71; Training groom, 38; Travelling paupers, 15; Vicars, 34, 74; Weaver, 67; Wheelwright, 72; Whitesmith, 50, 67; Yeoman, 30, 66-8, 70.
Outhwaite: family, 66, 68, 70; Anthony, 20; George, 20; James, 30; John, 28; Matthew, 67; Ralph, 17, 39, 66; Reginald, 28; Robert, 17, 20, 66.
Osborne: family, 15, 38, 39; Jane, 38; John, 27, 38, 70; John Howe, 38, 47; Mrs, 60.
Oxford, 46.
Oxgang, 9, 30.

Parish: Bellerby, 10, 46, 71; Council, 38; Registers, 15, 42.
Park Gill, 8, 68.
Pattison, Richard, 38; William, 72.
Peacock: family, 15; Richard, 15, 22, 30.
Pen Hill, 2, 15, 40.
Phillips, J. H., 46.
Pickersgill: family, 15; Joseph, 37, 67; Miles, 67.
Pinfold, 35.
Plant, Edward, 38.
Plews: Christopher, 22; Jane, 57; John, 28; Thomas, 28.
Poor Law provision, 22, 36-7.
Ploughlands, 4, 9-10, 20.
Pope, The, 40.
Population, 5, 18-9, 70.
Postal Service, 71.
Pratt: Issabell, 28; John, 28; William, 28.
Preest, Adam, 7.
Prehistory, 1-5.
Preston, Mr, 18.
Preston under Scar, 3-4, 10, 73, 79.
Probate records, 17-18, 20-1, 29, 39, 66.
Proctor, J., 27.
Pullan, J., 57, 74.

Quakers, 50-1, 54-5, 67.
Quarries: Black Beck, 2, 71; Deer Park, 68-9; Gilbert Scar, 56; Grey Greet, 2, 71; Halfpenny House, 47; Mains, 23; Moor Road, 2, 23, 37; Preston under Scar, 73.
Queen Anne's Bounty, 42.

Raby, John, 28.
Raper, Charles, 70.
Ravensworth, 28, 40.
Raw: and Hutchinson, 68; Francis, 37; George, 68; John, 33; James, 56; Leonard, 56; Thomas, 68.
Redcar, 60.
Redmire, 50, 71, 78-9.
Reeth, 27, 79.
Refugees, 63, 76.
Richardson, James, 71.
Richmond, 2, 6-7, 27, 30, 42, 50-1, 70.
Richmondshire, 2, 28, 50.
Riddell family, 49.
Ridley: family, 15; Alice, 15; Ann, 15; Henry, 15; James, 38, 47; Jane, 38; William, 23, 31, 59.
Ripon and Richmond Chronicle, 25, 74.
Ripon Diocese, 43, 45-7.

Roads: Green Way, 31; Grinton, 32, 71; Hubriggs Lane, 37; Huntergate/stye, 7, 82; Mains Lane, 38, Mill Lane, 8, 62; Moor Road, 2, 23, 37, 79; Richmond, 31-2; Richmond and Lancaster Turnpike, 2, 23, 68; Runs Bank/Lane, 2, 9, 37, 42, 82; Skelton Lane, 22; Wynd, The, 1, 3.
Robinson: family, 53; Charles, 67; George, 67; Jerome, 18, 21; Leonard, 31; Mrs, 60, 62; Richard, 51; Stephen, 31; Thomas, 46.
Rodwell, John, 68.
Roman Catholics, 42, 49-50.
Rowntree: Richard, 38, 71; William, 72.
Rufus, Simon, 7.
Russel family, 53.
Ryder: family, 71; John, 67, Joseph, 71; Mr, 74.

Samson the Clerk, 40.
Saunders, Samuel, 71.
Scarborough, 63.
Scarth Nick, 3.
School: Bellerby, 17, 35, 56-65, 76, 78-9; Teachers' List, 64-5.
Scotland, 4-5, 7, 15, 21.
Scott: John, 14-5, 72; Raymond, 38; William, 68.
Scrafton: Christopher, 28; Robert, 28; Thomas, 28; William, 28.
Scrope: family, 6, 20, 49; Geoffrey, 28; Henry, 7, 28, 40; John, 7; Simon, 32-2.
Scroops Pits (Coal), 32.
Seeley, Mr, 57.
Settlement pattern, 4.
Shepherd: Gregory the, 5; Mr, 49.
Shops, 37, 56, 67, 70-1.
Siggiswick, Thomas, 28.
Simpson (Symson), family, 53; Agnes, 30; Christopher, 30, 50; Elizabeth, 17, 29, 30; Gerome, 29; John, 29; Robert, 29; Simon, 30.
Singleton, Joseph, 57.
Skelton, Henry, 67.
South Africa, 17.
Sowerby, William, 28.
Sparke, Robert, 28.
Speight, Harry, 70.
Spence: family, 53; Henry 52; Isabella, 17, 57; Isaac, 52; W., 52,
Spennithorne, 3-4, 7, 15, 18, 23, 30, 36-7, 40-42, 45, 49, 79.
Spennithorne, John, 5.
Sporting right and field sports, 32, 36, 61, 70.
Spring Gill, 10, 23, 31, 82.
Stainton, 3-4, 10, 32.
Stephenson, Harry, 33.
Stewart, Mr, 27.
Stirk, Robert, 27, 47.
Stockell, Wm, 68.
Stockings, 56.
Storey family, 53; John, 67.
Strips and lynchetts, 9-10.
Summers: Richard, 33; Thomas, 53.
Sunday Schools, 52-3, 56, 61.
Sunderland, 63.
Sutton, Captain, 31.
Swaledale, Swale river, 2, 7, 40.
Swales, Thomasin, 32.
Swarthbeck (Black Beck), 10.
Sword Dance, 75.

Tarn, The, 7.
Tate, James, 42, 44.
Taxes, 4-5, 18.
Temperance, 52-3, 74.
Temple, William, 72.
Terry, Adam, 28; Ralph, 68.
Tervinne (stream), 6-7.
Thistlethwaite: family, 14, 71; Henry. 68; Herbert, 17; John, 68; Margaret, 17; William, 38.
Thompson, Thomas, 68.
Thornborough: family, 49.
Thorsby: family, 49; Peter, 5.
Tidyman: family, 15; Christopher, 72; Henry, 56-7; Mary, 57, 71; Thomas, 71.
Tindale, George, 56.
Tithe and the tithe barn, 7, 23, 42.
Tofts and crofts, 9.

Topham: Christopher, 37, Thomas, 38.
Tournament of Song, 63.
Township of Bellerby, 3-4, 7, 37.

Uldale, Ulvedale (Spring Gill), 10, 31, 82.
Ure river, 2, 40.
Ulshaw, 49.

Visitiations, 42, 45, 49, 52, 56.
Wade, Richard, 26.
Waite: family, 49; James, 49.
Walburn, 3-4, 6, 10, 22-3, 31, 53.
Walker: family, 53; Mr C, 52; Francis, 15, 17, 34, 47, 56-7; Thomas, 30; John, 37; William, 36; Mr, 52.
Walter, Brother, 10.
War, 63-4, 76, 78-9.
Warde: family, 53; Henry, 21.
Wardell, William, 27.
Watson, John, 71.
W E A, 78.
Weather, 5, 26-7, 60, 63-4.
Webster: family, 15; Matthew, 66.
Wederell (Wetherald): family, 67; Christopher, 21; Henry, 15; William, 15.
Wensley, 3, 79.
Wensleydale, 2, 3, 5, 7, 30, 50, 54, 58.
Wensleydale Advertiser, 46, 54.
Wensleydale Railway, 72.
Wesley, John, 50.
West Burton, 79.
Westmorland, 21.
West Witton, 46.
West Yorkshire, 4.
Whicham, Cumberland, 45.
Whitby, William, 28.
White, Charles A., 15, 47.
Whitelock, Robert, 71.
Whit Fell, 2, 32, 38, 40.
Whitfield, Thomas, 57.
Whitley Bay, 63.
Whorlton, 57.
Wilkinson: D. M., 62.
Willis, John, 28.
Wilson: Christopher, 28; John, 28.
Winne, James, 15.
Wood, Jane, 71.
Woodhouse, Grove, (School), 52.
Woodward: family, 53.
Wray, John, 70-1.
Wright: George, 23, 31-2; Mr, 74; Thomas, 31.
Wyvill: family, 49; Francis, 15; Marmaduke Asty, 36; Mr, 18.

Yarker, John, 36.
Yorebridge School, 42.
York, Archbishop of, 41.
Yorkshire Evening Post, 76.
Yorkshire Museum, 3.
Yorkshire Post, 76.
Yeadon, David, 68.